Dog-Gone Good
Cuisine

ALSO BY GAYLE PRUITT AND JOE GRISHAM

The Dog-Gone Good Cookbook

Dog-Gone Good Cuisine

More Healthy, Fast, and Easy Recipes for You and Your Pooch

Gayle Pruitt

Photographs by Joe Grisham

St. Martin's Griffin
New York

Photo credits: Joe Grisham, Photographer; Janet Healey, Art Director

www.stmartins.com

Design by Susan Walsh

The Library of Congress Cataloging-in-Publication Data is available upon request.

ISBN 978-1-250-03713-8 (trade paperback)
ISBN 978-1-250-03714-5 (e-book)

St. Martin's Griffin books may be purchased for educational, business, or promotional use. For information on bulk purchases, please contact Macmillan Corporate and Premium Sales Department at 1-800-221-7945, extension 5442, or write specialmarkets@macmillan.com.

First Edition: February 2014

10 9 8 7 6 5 4 3 2 1

I dedicate Dog-Gone Good Cuisine
to my two faithful companions,
Mimi and Mister Casper.

Contents

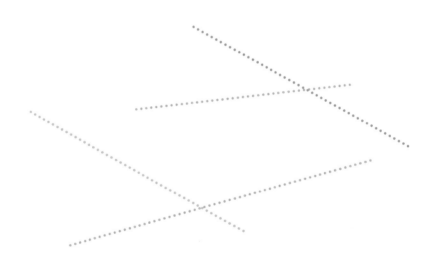

Acknowledgments

From Gayle Pruitt: First of all, I would like to thank Chancey Blackburn for her tireless effort in helping me with every aspect of this book. I will be forever grateful to my amazing agent, Linda Langton, who believed in this project from the very beginning. My sincere appreciation goes to Daniela Rapp, editor for St. Martin's Press, who took my words and recipes and made them into a cookbook. I also want to thank photographer Joe Grisham, his artist wife, Janet Healey, and set director, Keith Johnston. Each of their gorgeous photographs of food and dogs are works of art.

I would like to acknowledge two important people in my life, Rick and Lavonne Bradford, owners of the Sunflowers Shoppe in Fort Worth, Texas. Rick and Lavonne believed in my philosophy on food and opened the door to a world of nutrition for me. Without them this book would never have been written.

From Joe Grisham: To my wife and creative partner, Janet Healey, THANK YOU for always making work together so exciting. Your incredible ideas and brilliant vision never cease to amaze me!

Big thanks to Keith Johnston for your wonderful production design and styling. Also, thank you Katy Yost and Veronica Ramos for your help in the kitchen and keeping us on track every day.

Special appreciation to Art Ortiz of DogFit Dallas for your innovative dog wrangling. On set and off, all the dogs love you.

Susan Hubenthal, thank you for your witty chalkboard art and signage. You're a fabulous artist.

Finally, thank you to the extraordinary rescue dogs who showed up at our studio and gave us their all…just for some love and a few delicious treats. You're what keeps us going!

Foreword

It gives me great pleasure to be writing the foreword to *Dog-Gone Good Cuisine.* I can't remember a time in my life when I didn't have a dog as a companion. Some of my earliest memories revolve around my first dog, Penny, and ever since I have been the proud companion of a dog—even in medical school and residency when there wasn't an ounce of time to spare, I always made room for my dog/child.

Today, I work in private practice and am fortunate enough to be able to bring Remington, my beagle, to the office with me. He is a great source of joy for the patients (and the staff, too). He is the cutest and best dog on the planet (yes, I know, so is yours) and he brings an immediate smile to my patients' faces. Somehow what is bothering them becomes a little easier to bear. The simple act of a dog looking into your eyes can warm your soul and, scientifically, can help to boost your immune system.

As you can tell, I feel that dogs are a wonderful species and do so much for us that it is our important responsibility to manage their health. This brings me to the second reason why I am honored to be a part of this book. I am a medical doctor who specializes in nutritional medicine. I am very proactive with my human patients and do not wait for them to get sick, but encourage them to do something that positively affects their lives each day. This belief translates directly to the care of dogs.

For the most part, pet food is filled with things I wouldn't feed my worst enemy, let alone the one being that I love the most in the world. Gayle has really taken the lead in bringing to light the similarities in the way we can eat together with our dogs. She has created healthy delicious recipes that will impact your dog's health in a positive way and that are easy to prepare. I especially enjoy how varied and easy the recipes are—many of which I would never have thought of.

There are more than 100 recipes in this book, many of which will address human and canine lifestyle illnesses such as cancer, heart disease, diabetes, kidney issues, and liver disease and with special sections on fats, oils, herbs, and spices. You can see Gayle has love both for dogs and their owners as well as a commitment to cooking with healthful ingredients. Her passion is deep and her skill amazing.

Just as humans are plagued with obesity and degenerative illnesses such as arthritis, so are our canine friends. This is wrong and the only way to address the problem is to go to the root cause, which is what we feed our dogs. It disheartens me when I bring Remington to the vet and see all of the obese dogs or the ones with arthritis and the medications they are on. I just want to scream and tell the owners it doesn't have to be this way—you are killing your pet! Instead, I sit there and recommend Gayle's book.

A remarkable transformation has taken place in the human world in the past decade, where we are paying much more attention to the quality of the food we place in our mouths and acknowledge food's importance to our health and well-being. I am so pleased to see this transformation now extending to our pets.

Remington only gets raw vegetables for a treat and he loves them. His digestion is amazing, he never has diarrhea and his coat is extremely soft. This and more can all be achieved through good nutrition. Your dog doesn't have to be sick, and if he is, this book will quite possibly save his life.

—FRED PESCATORE, MD,
MPH, CCN

Introduction

Mom and Dad bought me an Easy-Bake oven when I was five years old. I was hooked and I've loved to cook ever since. They also always had a large garden; the vegetables were so fresh, so good, and so very healthy! Okra, black-eyed peas, green beans, and luscious red ripe tomatoes were picked right out of the garden to use for dinner. Mom would walk down to the creek and pick watercress to throw in salads. My grandmother also had an herb garden, so mint and basil were always on the table.

Many years later when I was working at a health food store, the store owners asked me if I would like to get my certification in nutrition. I jumped at the chance. I will always appreciate Rick and Lavonne Bradford, owners of Sunflower Shoppes in Fort Worth, Texas, a wonderful couple, for opening this door for me. It was the beginning of my quest for knowledge on how to use the right foods at the right time.

In our family we also always had animals, mainly dogs, but we had other strange critters, too. We had a raccoon that would pull open every drawer in the house if we left him alone, and would wash his apples in the sink; a pet goat named Feebee that played hide-and-seek with me; and a little ram named Bucky—my brother was afraid of him and that delighted me.

My grandmother guessed early on that I had a special affiliation with animals. I was about six when she handed me a sliced aloe plant and told me that a wild cat had her paw caught in a trap in the back field and had chewed her paw off. She told me to find the cat and doctor her. Funny, that wild cat found me, and let me put the aloe on her paw. She lived and brought her many kittens to my bedroom window and let me play with her babies.

So it's no surprise that I realized that health, food, and animals were my passions, and that I could put them all together in a book.

Mimi and Casper are the dogs in my life now. They give me love and enjoyment every day. They inspired me to write this cookbook. This book fulfills my need to give love and caring to them and to share it with all their buddies—human and furry.

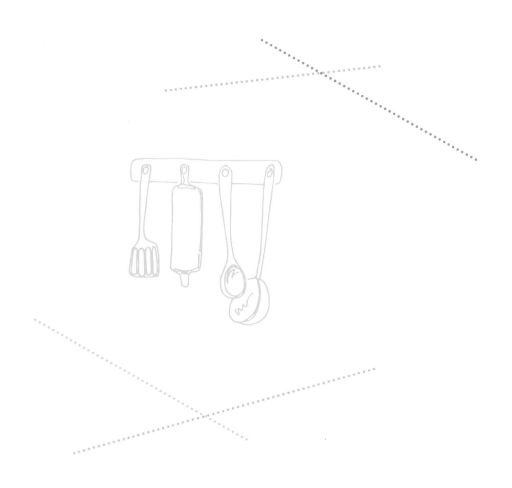

Gayle Pruitt

Why Cook (for Your Family and Your Dog)?

Of course your dog is part of your family, or at least I hope you feel that way. Dogs give us so much pleasure, love, and companionship and they help us in so many ways, if we allow them to do so. They can protect us, warn us of danger, make us smile, comfort us when we're lonely, and make us get up and exercise. I could go on and on. Dogs have been a part of the human culture for at least 25,000 years and probably much longer.

Good food is basic to good health. You can love your children and your dogs, but if the kids are eating at fast-food restaurants 70 percent of the time, and your dog is eating cheap, grain-filled, moldy food, then the instances of illnesses for both of them can increase threefold or more.

Research shows that children who have regular home-cooked meals and regularly eat with their families are healthier, fewer suffer from obesity, and they are less likely to get in trouble with the law. Likewise, a balanced, homemade varied diet for your dog keeps your dog healthy, happy, and out of the veterinarian's office. Besides, your dog deserves it.

So make time to prepare homemade meals for your family and for Fido, too. It's good for everyone's health!

Waste Not Want Not

My grandmother—we called her Mama—would always say "Don't throw those peelings away; we can use them." She showed me how to keep vegetable peelings and cuttings to make stock and how to make soup from leftovers that I was about to throw away. When I would cut the fat off the meat before I cooked it, she would say, "Don't throw the fat away; I'm going to use it."

I have had many lean years in my life and have put Mama's advice to practice, thankfully, so I always had enough food to make a healthy dinner for my family. Now that I cook for my dogs, some of my neighbors and their dogs, my brother who shows up for care packages, and for my son, I'm still glad Mama taught me to be frugal with food.

Below are a few general tips that have kept my family and my dogs eating well throughout the years:

- When buying meat in bulk, divide meats into smaller meal-size portions as soon as you get home from shopping. Store what you will be cooking first in the refrigerator and freeze the rest.
- When peeling or preparing vegetables on the "Good Veggie List" for dogs, save all the peelings and cuttings like carrot peels, celery tops, bell pepper tops, squash ends, and so forth and freeze them. Pull them out when making bulk dog food or a broth for either a soup for the family or maybe a gelatin for the dogs.
- When cooking a chicken, turkey, or some other meat that has bones, save the carcasses and the bones and freeze them. Do the same with the meat drippings. This makes a delicious healthy broth.

- When cutting fat from roasts, chicken, duck, or turkey, freeze the fat to render later. Rendered meat fat makes great flavoring for vegetables.
- Save squash and pumpkin seeds to either lightly roast for snacks or to use raw in bulk dog food.
- When juicing, save all the pulp for baking items such as high-fiber muffins, or for bulk dog food.
- If your family eats rice, quinoa, millet, or oats, cook up a large batch every two weeks and freeze in individual servings. That way all you have to do is defrost and add veggies and a protein.

These are just a few commonsense ideas, but they really help save time and money.

Equipment and Ingredients to Always Have on Hand

In the past I bought recipe books and I would often get in the middle of a great recipe and would not have the right equipment or all the right ingredients. I would have to improvise and it never came out the way the chef said it would and sometimes didn't even resemble the dish. However, I did create some different recipes (some good, some not so good). But having the correct equipment and ingredients will make your life so much easier.

Equipment

- Get a juicer; you won't be sorry. Presently there are inexpensive juicers on the market—some under $100. You can juice and freeze the fiber. You never know when you might need that bulk fiber for bulk dog food or maybe some high-fiber muffins.
- A food processor; there are inexpensive food processors (I use mine every day for so many kitchen jobs).
- A 15- to 20-quart enamel pot. If you're going to make the Turkey in a Pot recipe (page 29) or other bulk, high-quantity, canine-only recipes (and I highly recommend you do) you will need this. You can prepare enough bulk food to keep your furry kids happy for a while and there will also be enough to make several recipes for the human family, too. We don't want an aluminum pot, and a stainless steel pot is too expensive, so try a less expensive enamel pot. Be sure to also get a stainless steel steamer. That way you can put the steamer on the bottom of the pot so the chicken or turkey won't sit

on the bottom and burn. (I found out the hard way and ruined a 20-pound turkey and we couldn't even use the broth. I cried.)

- A large nontoxic, nonstick skillet
- Mini muffin pan
- Spatula (nonscratch)
- A good chef's knife with 8- to 10-inch blade
- Nontoxic freezer containers for individual servings of bulk dog food
- A meat grinder (optional). I don't use one, but for making a large amount of bulk dog food, it would be helpful.

Ingredients and Supplies

Chia seeds
Flaxseeds (I use sprouted)
Pumpkin seeds (raw)
Sunflower seeds (shelled, raw, no salt)
Coconut oil
Coconut flour
Shredded unsweetened coconut
Frozen peas
Frozen spinach
Frozen mixed vegetables (no onions, garlic, or beans)
Multivitamins and minerals (ask your vet)
Nutritional yeast
Lecithin (granules)
Cod liver oil, for canines
Missing Link supplement
Sea vegetables (nori, wakame, other types of kelp)
Bone meal

Eggs for omelets (you can use the shells for calcium)

Goat milk kefir

"Green Tripe" (optional), always good if you have a freezer in the garage—it stinks!

Vitamins and Minerals Used in Our Recipes

The foods in the recipes in this book are rich in the vitamins and minerals listed below. This is a limited outline of the many benefits and nutrients.

Vitamins

VITAMIN A

- Preformed Vitamin A is found in meat, poultry, and fish. Turkey liver is among the highest for finding Preformed Vitamin A.
- A small amount of liver is wonderful for your immune system. However, over-consumption of liver can be toxic and may lead to jaundice and even liver failure.
- Provitamin A is found in fruits, vegetables, and herbs. The most common type of Provitamin A in foods is beta-carotene. The body then has to convert the beta-carotene to Vitamin A to be able to utilize the A. Find Provitamin A in paprika, bell peppers (orange and yellow), sweet potatoes, carrots, winter squashes, lettuces, and dried herbs, such as parsley and basil.

VITAMIN B

B1 (thiamine)

B2 (riboflavin)

B3 (niacin)

B5 (pantothenic acid)

B6

B7 (biotin)

B12 and folic acid

B vitamins help your body make the energy from your foods. They help form red blood cells, reduce anemia, help prevent birth defects, help with depression, and may help reduce heart disease. We could write a whole book just on the B vitamins, but here is an overview.

Nutritional yeast is rich in all B vitamins and has all the amino acids. Millet and quinoa are also rich in B's and high in proteins. Other foods that contain the B's are:

	B12	
Asparagus		Caviar
Brussels sprouts		Cod
Butternut squash		Salmon
French green beans		Sardines
		Lamb
		Yogurt

VITAMIN C

Vitamin C helps to form collagen, which helps the body absorb iron. Vitamin C supports the body's structures and helps the formation of bones and teeth. Humans do not create their own Vitamin C; we need to consume it through foods rich in the vitamin or, in some cases, we need extra supplementation.

Dogs make their own Vitamin C, about 18mg per pound of weight. In the past it was not recommended to supplement a dog's diet with Vitamin C–rich foods or supplements. However, more and more evidence suggests that young puppies, older dogs, or dogs under stress due to lifestyle or chemicals in their environment would benefit from supplementation and eating Vitamin C–rich foods. Here are a few:

Bell peppers	Raspberries
Blueberries	Strawberries
Broccoli	Swiss chard
Brussels sprouts	

VITAMIN D3

Vitamin D is a fat-soluble vitamin and is best known for partnering with calcium to help build and maintain strong bones. Research has shown us the benefits of expanding Vitamin D3's role in maintaining the immune system. Though your body stores Vitamin D and can make it when your skin is exposed to sunlight, many of us just don't get out in the sun enough to make sufficient Vitamin D3 to keep us healthy.

Low levels of Vitamin D are linked to several different cancers, high blood pressure, depression, and obesity. Here are a few foods that include Vitamin D:

Caviar	Goat cheese
Cod	Sardines
Eggs	

VITAMIN E

Vitamin E helps prevent coronary heart disease, cognitive decline, age-related eye disorders, and even some cancers. Here are good sources of Vitamin E:

Blueberries	Raspberries
Butternut squash	Spirulina
Cranberries	Sunflower seed sprouts
Pumpkin	Swiss chard
Pumpkin seeds	

VITAMIN K

Vitamin K increases bone density and keeps calcium in the bones and away from the arteries. Vitamin K may also help protect us from certain brain diseases, and can be found in:

Asparagus	Broccoli	Cauliflower	Kale	Turkey (dark meat)
Beef	Brussels sprouts	Celery	Lamb	
Blueberries	Carrots	Cranberries	Raspberries	

Minerals

CALCIUM

Calcium is beneficial for the health and growth of bones. The body also needs calcium to help the nerves carry messages between the brain and the body. Calcium helps blood vessels to move blood through the body and works with hormones and enzymes that affect most functions in the body.

A dog that has enough calcium has a healthy coat, bones, nails, and teeth. A deficit of calcium could cause bone disease, osteoporosis, and heart problems for humans and dogs. Find calcium in:

Bonemeal (more phosphorus)
Canned salmon
Canned sardines
Eggshell calcium (lower phosphorus)
Leafy green vegetables such as kale, collard greens, and broccoli
Sea vegetables
Yogurt

CHLORIDE

Chloride functions as an electrolyte. It literally helps keep the body from drying up, maintains the pH balance in the blood, and helps remove carbon dioxide (CO_2) from the body. Chloride works in conjunction with sodium. Foods high in chloride include:

Celery
Lettuce
Tomatoes

IODINE

Iodine is an essential trace mineral that is important for correct thyroid function. The right amount of iodine helps the thyroid to regulate the body's metabolism, growth, and development in addition to many other thyroid functions. Sources of iodine:

Cranberries

Kombu

Organic goat milk kefir

Organic strawberries

Wakame

IRON

The health benefits of iron include carrying oxygen to human blood cells. Iron deficiency leads to anemia. Iron is also essential in the chemical reaction that helps change food into energy. Sources of iron include:

Beef

Eggs

Lamb

Liver

Salmon

Tuna

MAGNESIUM

For importance, magnesium should be right up there with air and water. Magnesium is required for more than 300 biochemical reactions in the body, including the healthy functioning of the muscles, heart, and kidneys. It helps stabilize the heartbeat, and is given to patients with heart arrhythmia. Find magnesium in these foods:

Kefir

Leafy green vegetables

Pumpkin seeds

Sea vegetables

Yogurt

PHOSPHORUS

Phosphorus improves protein formation, balances hormones, helps form healthy bones, helps with digestion and with cell repair, as well as many additional functions. Phosphorus is the second most abundant mineral in the body. Find phosphorus in these foods:

Beef	Gelatin
Bonemeal (more phosphorus)	Lamb
Gelatin	Peas
Eggshell calcium (less phosphorus)	Poultry
Fish	

POTASSIUM

Potassium helps with blood pressure, heart rate, and the nervous system. It also helps improve oxygen intake for the brain and helps neutralize acids in the joints, which benefits arthritis sufferers. These foods are good sources of potassium:

Broccoli	Sea vegetables
Collard greens	Spinach
Kale	Tomatoes

SELENIUM

Selenium is an antioxidant and plays an important role in maintaining a healthy immune system. It also helps with the regulation of thyroid hormones. Find selenium in these foods:

Brazil nuts (very high)	Fish
Chicken	Red meat
Eggs	

Zinc is another mineral that has many uses including aiding proper digestion, helping control diabetes, and the proper functioning of the immune system. It helps metabolize energy.

Zinc is used for acne, eczema, weight loss, and plays a big role in helping maintain brain health. It is also necessary in the metabolism of melatonin. Find zinc in these foods:

Lamb   Roast beef (low-fat)

Pumpkin seeds   Squash seeds

Superstars in the Herb and Spice World

Herbs and spices not only enhance you and your dog's enjoyment of eating; they may also help prevent disease or may even help the healing of some conditions.

There are herbs that increase immune function, lower blood pressure, regulate blood sugar, protect and help heal the liver, and may help prevent some forms of cancer. Wow!

And that's not all. Some herbs and spices might strengthen the heart and even help you and your little overweight furry buddy lose weight and increase energy levels. Can plants really do all that? I say "Yes they can and much more."

When I first adopted Mimi, she was very nervous and had many digestive issues including diarrhea, vomiting, and flatulence. My sweet Mimi ruined the bedroom carpet. I had to replace the carpet with a wood laminate. That's when I started adding a little fresh ginger and dried fennel seeds to her food and the improvement in her digestion was almost immediate. Plus she really liked the taste. When Casper came into our life, his skin was inflamed. The ginger and the turmeric helped alleviate a big portion of his inflammation.

I've listed a few of the top stars in the herb and spice world that I use in my

recipes along with some of their possible benefits for you and your dog. Adding a little spice to your dog's food is a way to say I love you.

Herbs Safe for Both Humans and Dogs

1. Parsley has anti-inflammatory and antioxidant properties and may help to eliminate certain toxins in the body. It is also great for the digestive system and cleans up the liver. Parsley helps relieve gas and also helps with expelling parasites.

    There is a compound in parsley and celery seeds called apiol, which is used in some medications to help with certain kidney conditions. This combination may help with gout and other forms of arthritis.
2. Dill is chemoprotective and has bacteriostatic properties. In other words, it protects us against harmful chemicals and bacteria. Dill is also considered a good source of calcium. Kayla, a little prissy poodle who lives next door, loves a little dill in her food.
3. Basil is a rich source of antioxidants beta-carotene, cryptoxanthin, lutein, and zeaxanthin. These antioxidants fight against age-related diseases.
4. Fennel bulb is a good source of Vitamin C, fiber, and manganese. It is also rich in potassium, magnesium, calcium, iron, and Vitamin B3. The fiber from fennel helps eliminate carcinogens and toxins.

    Dried fennel seeds help both you and your dog's digestion. It also helps with stomach pains and infantile colic; however, the seeds of fennel should only be used in small amounts.

Spices Safe for Both Humans and Dogs

1. Turmeric has an active ingredient called curcumin. The spice has been used for over 2,500 years, maybe longer. Scientific research has shown that turmeric is beneficial for many conditions including everything from Alzheimer's disease to some cancers. I do not have enough room to list all

the benefits of this amazing spice, but listed below are a few of its many uses.

Turmeric is a natural antiseptic and antibacterial agent. When you combine turmeric with certain cruciferous vegetables it has been shown to help stop the growth of prostate cancer. Turmeric may cause certain cancer cells to commit suicide.

It may lower the risk of Alzheimer's by removing amyloyd plaque buildup in the brain. It is a natural anti-inflammatory that works, possibly better than some anti-inflammatory drugs, but without the side effects. Turmeric may also help with weight management. So give your pooch some turmeric sprinkled in his food every once in a while…it's oh so good.

2. Clove is one of the spices that is the most powerful in antioxidants, and has been well-known for thousands of years to have germicidal properties that help fight infections, and relieve digestive problems and arthritis pain. Clove oil has been used to help with the pain of toothaches, and it helps rid dogs of worms.

3. Ginger outperforms all other spices in its many uses, from flavoring great food to benefiting health. Ginger helps relieve gas, nausea, and vomiting—and is especially helpful during pregnancy. It is very effective in preventing the symptoms of motion sickness, especially seasickness. Ginger has been shown to be more effective than Dramamine in some cases. Plus it's an anti-inflammatory. Ginger's active component, *gingerol,* has anti-inflammatory compounds, which appear to help with the pain in osteoarthritis or rheumatoid arthritis. Gingerols may help slow the growth of cancer cells in the colon and it may help induce cell death in many other cancer cells. And it's great in recipes!

4. Fenugreek—I have taken fenugreek along with thyme for hay fever for years and it works wonders, but it also has a myriad of other uses. Fenugreek has been found to lessen the effects of hot flashes and PMS. It has also been used to treat asthma, bronchitis, and improve digestion.

Recently fenugreek has been shown to help regulate blood sugar levels and it may lower blood glucose, which could help make it an effective treatment for diabetes. And, it's delicious!

5. Cinnamon—oh my, all the wonderful things I can say about cinnamon! Actually, I could write a whole book just about this one multifaceted spice.

Cinnamon tastes sweet and smells great. It has been used through the centuries for diabetes, arthritis, and infections. Cinnamon helps to regulate blood sugar levels. Because of its anti-inflammatory properties it eases pain and stiffness in joints. Cinnamon has antimicrobial, antibacterial, and antifungal properties. The anticlotting and anti-inflammation properties may help improve blood circulation.

Remember to *use only small amounts* of these herbs and spices and you will see powerful results for you and Fido. And always consult your veterinarian when using new ingredients.

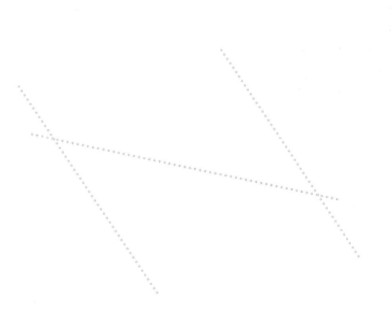

Basic Techniques

In this chapter, there are directions for making homemade chicken, beef, and vegetable broths. I recommend filtered water for all of these recipes; in fact, I recommend using filtered water anytime you cook. I also explain how to prepare a basic brisket, make turkey in a pot, and prepare brown rice, quinoa, and millet.

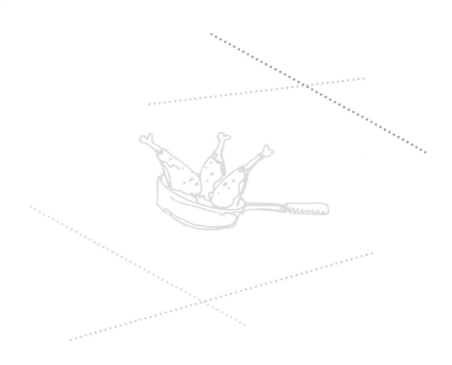

Boney Chicken or Turkey Carcass Broth

Ingredients

    2 chicken carcasses or 1 turkey carcass, reserved and frozen from a prior meal

    3 quarts water

    2 tablespoons Bragg Apple Cider Vinegar

    3 carrots, washed and coarsely chopped

    2 celery stalks, coarsely chopped

Add carcass, water, and vinegar to a large pot and let sit for at least 1 hour. Add the remaining ingredients, place on burner, and bring to a boil. Reduce heat and simmer for 3 hours.

The vinegar pulls the calcium out of the bones and into the broth.

Boney Beef Broth

Ingredients

 5 pounds beef marrow bones (usually found in meat section of the grocery store freezer)

 3 quarts water

 2 tablespoons Bragg Apple Cider Vinegar

 3 carrots, washed and coarsely chopped

 2 stalks celery, coarsely chopped

Add bones, water, and vinegar to a large pot and let sit for at least 1 hour. Add remaining ingredients, place on burner over high heat, and bring to a boil. Reduce heat and simmer, uncovered, for 3 hours.

The vinegar pulls the calcium out of the bones and into the broth.

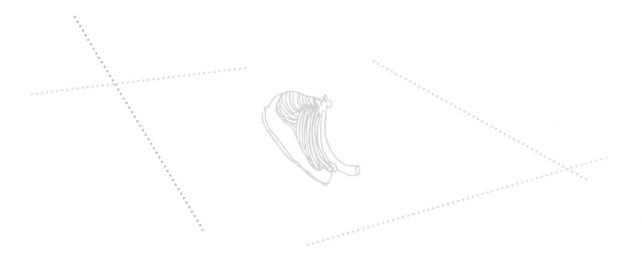

Meaty Beef Broth

Ingredients

5 pounds beef marrow bones (Usually found in the meat section of grocery store freezer)

½ pound stew meat

Reserved liquid from a roast (optional)

½ pound carrots, coarsely chopped

2 tablespoons coconut oil, melted

2 to 3 stalks of celery, coarsely chopped

1 to 2 green peppers, chopped (optional)

3 bay leaves

Preheat oven to 400 degrees. On a large baking sheet, place bones, stew meat, reserved liquid if using, carrots, and oil, and bake uncovered for about 35 minutes, until the meat starts to brown. Transfer the bones, meat, and carrots into a large 16-quart stockpot. Place the baking sheet on a burner and deglaze with a cup of water. Scrape all the brown bits and pour into the stockpot.

Fill the stockpot with cold water, 2 inches over the top of the bones. Add the remaining ingredients. Cook over high heat until the liquid starts to boil. Reduce heat, cover pot, and simmer for about 5 hours. Let the broth cool, then strain it, discarding the bones and vegetables, leaving only the broth. After the broth has cooled completely, freeze in individual freezer bags or containers.

Good idea: Name and date each bag with a marker or a label.

Homemade Vegetable Broth

Ingredients

- 3 quarts water
- 2 carrots, washed and coarsely chopped
- 3 stalks of celery, coarsely chopped
- 1 bell pepper, any color, coarsely chopped
- 4 medium zucchini or yellow squash, coarsely chopped
- ½ cup parsley, loosely packed, chopped
- 2 fresh bay leaves
- 1 teaspoon thyme (or any other favorite herb)

Add all ingredients to a large pot and cook for 3 hours on medium-low heat. Strain broth and let cool, then discard vegetables. You may want to freeze in small servings.

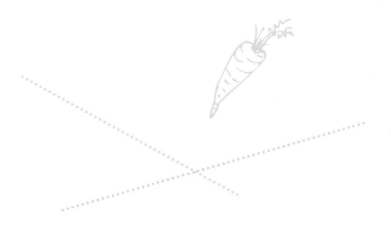

Basic Brisket

Here are the basic directions to prepare any brisket: Before cooking, trim the fat off the top of brisket, leaving about a ¼-inch layer.

Ingredients

> 1 (6- to 7- pounds) beef brisket
> 2 teaspoons dried thyme leaves
> 1½ teaspoons Celtic Sea Salt
> 1½ pounds carrots, peeled and sliced into 2-inch coins
> 4 celery stalks, cut into 2-inch pieces
> 3 or 4 bay leaves
> 1 bottle Lakewood Organic Super Veggie Juice (the only bottled juice I've found with no onions)

Preheat the oven to 325 degrees.

Place the brisket in a glass or ceramic rectangular ovenproof dish. Rub the thyme and salt on the meat.

Add the carrots, celery, and bay leaves, placing them around the brisket, and pour in enough veggie juice to come about halfway up the meat and vegetables. Cover the top of the dish with parchment paper, then with aluminum foil. Do not let tomato juice touch the foil; it will cause an unwanted chemical reaction, which will erode the foil and allow bits of aluminum to migrate into the food, which can leave a metallic taste in the mouth.

Bake for 4 to 4½ hours until the meat is tender.

Remove the meat from the dish and keep it warm. Continue to cook the vegetables and sauce in the oven, uncovered, for another 15 to 20 minutes until the sauce thickens.

Once the brisket has rested for 15 minutes, slice the meat against the grain.

Remove the vegetables from the sauce and transfer to a platter. Remove and discard the bay leaves. Arrange the sliced meat over the vegetables, pour a little sauce over the meat, and serve.

Serves 12 to 15

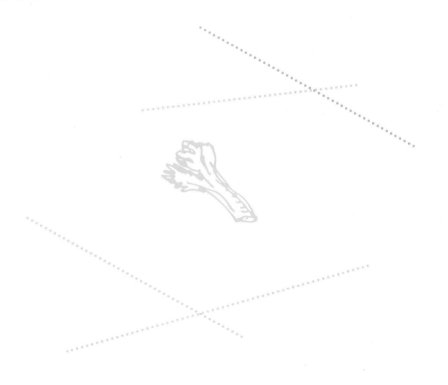

Turkey in a Pot

Ingredients

1 (12- to 15-pound) whole turkey (or 20-pound if you are adventurous), thawed

5 bay leaves

5 medium carrots, cut into several pieces

5 celery stalks, cut into several pieces

Water

Put the thawed turkey in a large pot along with the bay leaves, carrots, and celery. If using an enamel pot, place a stainless steel steamer on bottom of pot so the turkey won't burn. Cover the turkey with water and place the pot over high heat. Once the water comes to a boil, reduce the heat to a simmer. Cover the pot and let cook for 90 minutes. Check for doneness; the turkey meat should be coming off the bone. Remove the turkey and cool, then remove the meat from the bones. Strain the broth and discard the bay leaves and the vegetables.

How to Cook Brown Rice, Quinoa, and Millet

Here is some basic information for cooking brown rice, quinoa, and millet to serve to your canine.

When cooking rice, quinoa, or millet, the general rule is 1 part rice, quinoa, or millet to 2 parts liquid. However, for better digestion for canines, I have adjusted the normal ratios.

For rice, use 1 part rice to 2½ parts liquid. For quinoa or millet, use 1 part to 2¼ parts liquid. Also, cook for 10 minutes longer than the recipe calls for.

Brown Rice

Ingredients
    1 cup brown rice
    2½ cups water or other liquid
    1 tablespoon coconut oil or olive oil

In a large pot, warm the oil over medium heat. Add the rice and stir to coat all the grains with the oil. Add the liquid and let it come almost to a boil, then reduce the heat to low. Cover and cook for 45 minutes to 1 hour. Fluff with a fork.

Quinoa

....

Ingredients

    1 cup quinoa

    2¼ cups water

    1 tablespoon coconut oil or olive oil

In a large pot, warm the oil over medium heat. Add the quinoa and stir to coat all the grains with the oil. Add the water and let it come almost to a boil. Reduce the heat to low, cover, and cook for 30 to 35 minutes.

Millet

....

Ingredients

    1 cup millet

    2¼ cups water

    1 tablespoon coconut oil or olive oil

In a large pot warm the oil over medium heat. Add the millet and stir to coat all the grains with oil. Add the water and let it come almost to a boil. Reduce the heat to low, cover, and cook for 30 to 35 minutes.

Human/Canine

Breakfasts

Plain Chia and Flaxseed Pancake

Dry Ingredients

    ¼ cup gluten-free, all-purpose flour

    1 teaspoon chia seeds

    1 teaspoon flax meal

Wet Ingredients

    1 large egg

    ¼ cup water

    1 tablespoon butter or coconut oil

In a medium bowl combine all the dry ingredients and mix well. In a separate bowl, whisk together the egg and water.

Put the butter in the skillet and place over medium–high heat.

Add the wet ingredients to the bowl with the dry ingredients and stir until just mixed. Be careful not to overmix.

When the skillet is hot, and the butter has stopped foaming, spread the butter evenly over the bottom of the skillet, using a pastry brush. Pour the pancake batter into the hot skillet, spread out evenly, and reduce the heat to medium. Cook for about 8 minutes, then gently lift the pancake with a spatula to see if it is golden brown and will flip easily. When it is ready, carefully flip the pancake and let it cook on the opposite side for another 3 to 4 minutes until cooked through.

Strawberry-Basil Chia Jam (inspired by Jessica Griffin, N.C.)

Ingredients

16 ounces fresh organic
strawberries

¼ cup chia seeds

15 to 20 fresh basil leaves
(about ¾ ounce)

1 tablespoon water

Place all the ingredients in a food processor or blender and process, leaving some strawberries in small chunks. Refrigerate overnight.

For humans only: Add a little stevia to the jam.

CHA-CHA-CHA CHIA

Chia for you and your best furry furry Bud.

Chia seeds have just about everything: complete protein, the richest source of omega-3 fatty acids in the plant world, and 25 percent fiber. But wait—that's not all! Chia is high in calcium, magnesium, and zinc. And there's more—chia seeds can absorb up to 12 times their weight in liquid so they are great for keeping the body hydrated.

Chia is native to central and southern Mexico and Guatemala, and Native Americans have said that 1 tablespoon of chia could sustain a warrior for up to 24 hours. Chia seeds have little flavor so they're wonderfully versatile. You can use them in savory dishes, desserts, and even breads.

The recipes below are easy and superhealthy for all of us, including adults, kids, and dogs.

Basic Omelet

....

Ingredients
  2 large eggs
  1 teaspoon water
  1 teaspoon coconut oil

Dash of mild paprika

Place the eggs in a mixing bowl with the water and whisk with either a fork or small whisk.

Heat a 6- to 8-inch omelet pan or a rounded nonstick skillet over high heat until very hot, 20 to 30 seconds. Add the coconut oil and, using a spatula, evenly coat the bottom of the pan.

As soon as the oil stops bubbling, pour the egg mixture into the pan. Tilt the pan to spread the egg mixture evenly over the pan. Let the mixture firm up a bit, then lift the sides up with a spatula to allow the remaining liquid to run onto the pan.

Let the mixture firm up again for a few seconds. Tilt the pan to one side and, using the spatula, fold about one-third of the omelet over the middle.

Slide the omelet to the edge of the pan with the spatula. Hold the pan over the serving plate, and carefully roll the omelet off onto the plate. Sprinkle with paprika and serve.

Serves 1 human or 2 small to medium dogs

Omelet with Spinach and Goat Cheese

Ingredients

    2 large eggs

    1 teaspoon water

    1 teaspoon coconut oil

    Dash of mild paprika

Filling

    ¼ cup fresh baby spinach leaves

    4 to 5 fresh basil leaves (optional)

    1 tablespoon goat cheese

Crack the eggs into a mixing bowl, add the water, and whisk with either a fork or small whisk. Add the spinach leaves.

Heat a 6- to 8-inch omelet pan or rounded nonstick skillet over high heat until very hot, 20 to 30 seconds. Add the coconut oil and, using a spatula, evenly coat the bottom of the pan. As soon as the oil stops bubbling, add the basil leaves and pour the egg mixture over the leaves.

Tilt the pan to spread the egg mixture evenly over the pan. Let the mixture firm up a bit, then lift the sides up with a spatula to allow the remaining liquid to run onto the pan.

Let the mixture firm up again for a few seconds, then add the goat cheese to the middle of the omelet.

Tilt the pan to one side and, using the spatula, fold about one-third of the omelet over the goat cheese in the middle. Slide the omelet to the edge of the pan with the spatula. Hold the pan over the serving plate, and carefully roll the omelet onto the plate.

Sprinkle with paprika and serve.

Serves 1 human or 2 to 3 small to medium dogs

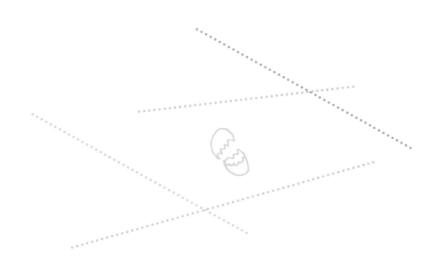

Appetizers

When having family or friends over for a formal or casual get-together, appetizers are a must. And in my dog-friendly household my guests are encouraged to bring their furry buddies along. So when I make my appetizers, they need to taste good, and be healthy for dogs and humans at the same time.

Veggie Snack Tray

Ingredients

    1 pound green beans

    4 medium carrots peeled, cut, and sliced into medium- size sticks

    4 ounces sugar snap peas, strings removed

    1 red bell pepper, seeded and julienned

    1 yellow bell pepper, seeded and julienned

    1 pint cherry tomatoes

Fill a bowl with ice and water. Set aside. Bring a pot of water to a boil. Add the green beans and blanch for 2 minutes. Add the carrots and boil for 3 minutes more. Add the sugar snap peas and cook for 30 seconds.

Shock the beans, carrots, and sugar snap peas in the bowl of ice water. Cool and drain.

To serve, arrange all the vegetables on a platter, placing the cherry tomatoes in the center, or place the veggies in individual containers for snacks.

For canines only: Dip the vegetables in chicken or beef broth (no onions).

Spinach Canapés with Almonds and Brazil Nuts

....

This recipe includes Brazil nuts. They are delicious and have some unusual aspects. They are extremely high in selenium. That means that Brazil nuts are great for the immune system. Be careful. Eating more than 3 or 4 nuts a day could result in selenium toxicity. Also, Brazil nuts can cause a reaction in some people that have other nut allergies. Dogs under 80 lbs should not exceed 2 nuts per day; under 50 lbs, 1 per day; under 30 pounds should not exceed ½ nut every two days.

Ingredients

Brazil nuts

1 (10-ounce) package frozen chopped spinach, cooked, cooled, and squeezed dry

1 (8-ounce) container mascarpone cheese

½ cup mayonnaise

½ cup almonds, finely chopped

3 Brazil nuts, finely chopped

½ teaspoon dried tarragon

2 medium cucumbers, sliced into ¼-inch rounds

2 medium yellow summer squash, sliced into ¼-inch rounds

2 medium zucchini, sliced into ¼-inch rounds

Thinly sliced roasted red pepper, chopped fresh dill, or halved, small grape tomatoes, for garnish

Combine the spinach, cheese, mayonnaise, chopped nuts, and tarragon. Chill in refrigerator for about 1 hour; you can make this the night before.

Fill a pastry bag with the mixture and pipe it onto the sliced cucumber, yellow squash, or zucchini. Garnish with the roasted red peppers, dill, or halved grape tomatoes.

Makes about 40 rounds

Roasted Red Pepper and Spinach Pancake with Goat Cheese

Dry Ingredients

    ¼ cup gluten-free, all purpose flour

    1 teaspoon chia seeds

    1 teaspoon flax meal

Wet Ingredients

    2 large eggs

    2 roasted red peppers, seeded and cut into strips (you may use jarred peppers)

    ¼ cup carrot juice, plus 1 tablespoon if needed

    1 teaspoon coconut oil

    5 or 6 baby spinach leaves

    ½ cup goat cheese

Combine all the dry ingredients in a bowl and mix well. In a separate bowl, whisk together the eggs, peppers, and carrot juice.

Add the coconut oil to a skillet over medium-high heat.

Add the wet ingredients to the bowl with the dry ingredients and stir until completely incorporated (you may add more carrot juice if the batter is too thick). Be careful not to overmix.

When the skillet is hot and the coconut oil has melted, spread the oil evenly over the bottom of skillet using a pastry brush. Spread the spinach leaves on the bottom of the skillet, pour the pancake batter over the leaves, and spread out evenly.

Reduce the heat to medium-low and cook for about 10 minutes. Gently lift up the pancake with a spatula to see if it is golden brown and will flip easily. When it is ready, carefully flip the pancake and let cook on the opposite side for about 4 minutes more, or until cooked through.

Serve the pancake with the spinach leaves facing up, and add a couple of dollops of plain goat cheese on top. Cut the pancake into pie-shape wedges. This is great for appetizers or just a great treat. Dogs will love these, and so will you.

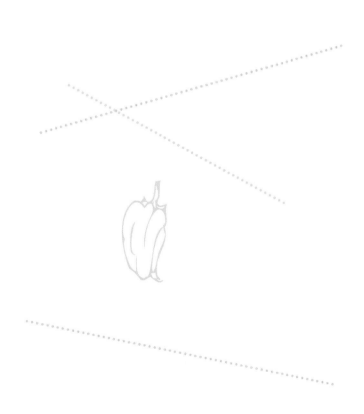

Soups

Classic Chicken Soup

Ingredients

(2- to 3-pound) whole chicken

2 quarts water

½ pound carrots, washed and coarsely chopped

½ pound carrots, peeled and sliced about 1 inch thick on the diagonal

3 celery stalks, coarsely chopped

2 celery stalks, strings removed, and sliced on the diagonal

2 bay leaves

Dash of Celtic sea salt

¼ cup parsley, finely chopped

Wash the chicken and place it in a large pot with the water, *chopped* carrots, *chopped* celery, bay leaves, and salt. Place over medium-high heat, cover, and cook for about 45 minutes, or until the meat starts coming off the bone.

Transfer the chicken to a platter to cool. Cook the broth another 30 to 40 minutes.

When cool enough to handle, remove the chicken meat from the bone and cut into cubes.

Strain the broth and return the strained broth to the pot. Add the *sliced* carrots and *sliced* celery.

Cook over medium-low heat until the carrots are easily pierced with a fork. Return the chicken meat to the pot, add the finely chopped parsley, and cook for 5 minutes more before serving. This soup freezes well.

Serves 4 to 6

Tomato-Carrot Soup

Ingredients

1 (15-ounce) can diced organic
    tomatoes
3 medium carrots, peeled and
    coarsely chopped
1 sweet potato, peeled and cut into
    4 to 5 slices
½ cup red lentils, rinsed and drained
1 quart water or vegetable broth
    (no onions)

3 medium carrots cut into ¼ x 2-inch
    sticks
12 grape-size tomatoes, halved
10 fresh basil leaves, chopped, plus
    5 whole basil leaves, cut into
    chiffonade, for garnish
Dash of Celtic sea salt
1 tablespoon extra-virgin olive oil

Add the tomatoes, carrots, potato, lentils, and water to a large pot and bring to a boil over medium-high heat. Reduce the heat to simmer and cook for about 25 minutes, or until the lentils and sweet potatoes are soft.

Using a handheld immersion blender or food processor, purée the soup until silky smooth.

Blanch carrot sticks in boiling water until barely soft. Shock in ice water and reserve for garnish. Add the tomatoes, chopped basil, and salt, stir, and cook for 3 minutes more. Stir in the olive oil.

Cut the whole basil leaves into a chiffonade. Stack the basil leaves and roll them into a tube, then cut across the ends of the rolled leaves to make little ribbons. Garnish the top of the soup with the blanched carrot sticks, sprinkle a few "ribbons" of basil over the carrot sticks, and serve.

Minestrone Soup

Ingredients

¼ cup olive oil

4 carrots, chopped

2 zucchini, thinly sliced

8 ounces green beans, cut into 1-inch pieces

4 celery stalks, thinly sliced

3 quarts chicken or vegetable broth (no onions)

6 kale leaves, roughly chopped

1 (15-ounce) can organic tomato sauce

1 pint cherry tomatoes, halved

2 tablespoons dried oregano

2 (15-ounce) cans cannellini beans with liquid (optional; some dogs have digestive issues caused by legumes)

Grated Parmesan or Pecorino Romano cheese, for garnish

Heat the olive oil in a large soup pot over medium heat and add the carrots, zucchini, green beans, celery, and stock. Cover, reduce the heat to low, and cook for 15 minutes, stirring occasionally.

Stir in the kale, tomato sauce, tomatoes, oregano, and cannellini beans with their liquid and bring to a boil. Cover, reduce the heat to low, and simmer for about 35 minutes.

Serve with the grated cheese.

Serves 10

Cream of Cinderella Pumpkin Soup

Ingredients

    1 Cinderella pumpkin

    2 tablespoons extra-virgin olive oil

    1 red bell pepper, seeded and finely chopped

    1 green bell pepper, seeded and finely chopped

    1 quart chicken broth (no onions)

    2 tablespoons heavy cream

    Dash of Celtic sea salt

Preheat the oven to 350 degrees.

Carefully cut off the top part of the pumpkin, then replace the top on the pumpkin. Put the pumpkin on a large baking sheet. (If you don't have one large enough, protect your oven by folding several sheets of heavy-duty aluminum foil, and covering the whole oven rack, making sure the foil is turned up slightly on the edges to catch any leakage from the pumpkin). Bake for about 30 minutes, then press on the skin of the pumpkin. If it gives a little, remove it from the oven.

Using a spoon, remove the seeds from the center of the pumpkin and reserve them for other recipes. Gently pull the flesh of the pumpkin off the inside and bottom, being careful not to break the skin. Set the hollowed pumpkin aside carefully.

Add 1 tablespoon of the oil to a skillet over medium-high heat. Add the onion, bell peppers, and garlic and sauté for about 5 minutes.

Add the chicken broth and the pumpkin flesh and cook for 10 minutes more.

Transfer the bell pepper and pumpkin mixture to a food processor and process until smooth. Add the cream and process for 30 seconds more. Season with salt to taste.

Pour the soup back into the pumpkin and serve. Delicious!

The instructions look harder than they are. You can use different kinds of seasonings —just experiment! (But no garlic or onion for Fido's version).

Serves 6 to 8

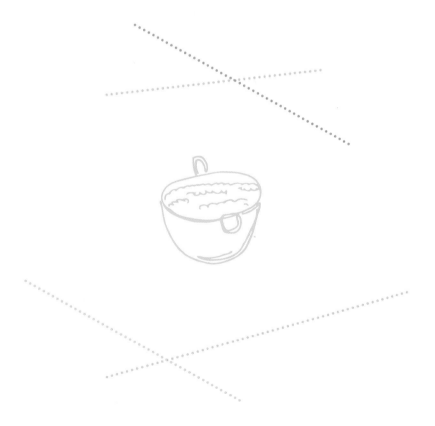

Beef
Entrées

Savory Brisket

Ingredients

    1 (3- to 4-pound) brisket, trimmed

    ½ teaspoon garlic powder (optional)

    1 tablespoon ground cumin

    1 teaspoon dried oregano

    2 teaspoons Celtic sea salt

    2 tablespoons olive oil

Preheat the oven to 275 degrees.

Mix the seasonings and salt together and rub all over the brisket.

Wrap the brisket in plastic wrap and refrigerate overnight.

Pour the oil into a glass or ceramic dish. Unwrap the brisket and place it on top of oil. Cover and cook in the oven for 5 hours.

Serves 6 to 8

Beef Stew with Spaghetti Squash

....

Ingredients

    1 large spaghetti squash

    1 tablespoon coconut oil

    1 (2- to 3-pound) chuck roast, cut in ½-inch cubes

    1 (15-ounce) can tomato sauce

    1 red bell pepper, seeded and coarsely diced

    1 green bell pepper, seeded and coarsely diced

    1 tablespoon herbes de Provence

    Dash of salt

Preheat the oven to 350 degrees.

Slice the spaghetti squash in half lengthwise and place it, cut side down, on a nonstick baking sheet. Bake for about 30 minutes, or until soft when poked with your finger. Set aside to cool.

In a hot skillet over medium heat, warm the coconut oil. Add and brown the beef cubes on all sides. Add the rest of the ingredients, cover, and cook for about 1½ hours over medium-low heat or until the beef is tender.

Remove the seeds from the squash and reserve them for another recipe. Shred the squash flesh with a fork into strands that look like spaghetti. Place the squash on plates and spoon the beef stew over the top.

Serves 4 to 6

Beef Kebabs

Ingredients

    1 pound beef sirloin, cut into pieces ½ inch thick and 1¼ inches long

    2 tablespoons olive oil

    1 teaspoon ground turmeric

    ½ red bell pepper, seeded and cut into 1-inch squares

    ½ yellow bell pepper, seeded and cut into 1-inch squares

    ½ green bell pepper, seeded and cut into 1-inch squares

    ½ teaspoon Celtic sea salt

    Bamboo skewers, soaked in water for 30 minutes

Mix the meat, 1 tablespoon of the olive oil, and the turmeric in a medium bowl. Let the meat come to room temperature, 30 to 45 minutes. Thread the meat onto skewers, about 5 pieces of meat per skewer. Then thread the peppers on separate skewers, 5 or 6 pieces per skewer. Brush all the skewers with the remaining 1 tablespoon olive oil, and season with salt.

Place all the skewers on baking sheet and broil for 6 to 7 minutes, turning during the process, or cook on hot grill for about 12 minutes, or until done. The veggie skewers will cook faster than the beef skewers.

Serve on a bed of lightly sautéed baby spinach and cherry tomatoes.

Serves 4

    Gayle Pruitt

Cooked Grass-Fed Chuck Roast with Green Beans and Tomato Sauce

Ingredients

   1 (2- to 3-pound) grass-fed chuck roast, cut in ½-inch cubes

   1 tablespoon coconut oil

   1 (15-ounce) can low-sodium organic tomato sauce

   1 red bell pepper, seeded and chopped

   1 pound French green beans (haricot verts), halved

   1 teaspoon dried oregano

Place cubed meat and coconut oil in skillet over medium–low heat. Cover and cook for 1 hour. Add the tomato sauce, oregano, and bell peppers and cook an additional 30 minutes more, or until the meat is tender. Lightly steam the green beans.

For Dogs: Put some steamed green beans in bowl with the proper amount of meat mixture and gently stir together.

For Humans: Season with salt and oregano or other spices to taste.

Serves 6 to 8

Curried Beef Sliders

Patties

    1¼ pound grass-fed ground beef (labeled 90 percent lean)

    1 teaspoon ground fenugreek

    ¼ teaspoon garlic powder

    ¼ teaspoon Celtic sea salt

    6 small gluten-free buns, lightly toasted

    1 tablespoon coconut oil

Curried Mayonnaise

    2 tablespoons organic mayonnaise

    ½ teaspoon ground fenugreek

    ½ teaspoon ground turmeric

Mix the ground beef, spices, and salt together and form 6 patties, about 3.3 ounces each. Warm the coconut oil in a skillet over medium-high heat. Add the patties and cook for 3 to 4 minutes on one side; turn and cook for 2 minutes on the opposite side, or until done.

To make curried mayonnaise, mix all the ingredients together in a small bowl. Spread the toasted gluten-free buns with the mayonnaise.

Build the sliders using soft lettuce, tomatoes, and the cooked patties.

Serves 6

Mediterranean Meatballs on a Stick

Ingredients

4 slices of Udi's, or other gluten-free bread

¼ cup chicken broth (no onions)

1½ pounds ground grass-fed beef (labeled 90 percent fat)

½ pound ground lamb

1 large egg

1 large bunch fresh flat-leaf parsley, finely chopped

1 teaspoon dried mint

½ teaspoon ground cinnamon

½ teaspoon powdered garlic (optional)

½ teaspoon Celtic sea salt

Preheat the oven to 350 degrees.

In a medium bowl, soak the bread in the chicken broth for a few minutes. Squeeze to remove excess moisture. Place the bread in a large bowl and, using your hands, mix together with the meat, egg, herbs, spices, and salt.

Form the mixture into 15 small balls. Brown the meatballs in a large skillet over medium heat.

Thread 3 meatballs on each skewer and set the skewers on a baking sheet.

Bake until just cooked through, 15 to 20 minutes.

Serve with a yogurt and mint sauce.

Serves 6 to 8

Spiced Stuffed Peppers

Ingredients

6 bell peppers (yellow and green)

1¼ pounds (labeled 90 percent lean) ground beef

1½ teaspoons coconut oil

1 teaspoon peeled and minced fresh ginger

½ teaspoon ground cinnamon

¼ teaspoon ground cloves

⅔ cup tomato purée

1 tablespoon apple cider vinegar

1 cup overcooked brown rice

Preheat the oven to 350 degrees.

Gently cut the tops off the bell peppers with a knife and set aside. Remove the seeds and membranes. Place the peppers, standing upright, in a shallow casserole dish with a ¼ inch of water. Bake for 15 minutes.

Meanwhile, sauté the meat in the coconut oil, along with the ginger, cinnamon, and cloves. When the meat is brown, about 10 minutes, add the tomato purée and vinegar and cook for 5 minutes more. Add the cooked rice.

Remove the peppers from the oven and stuff them with the meat mixture. Place the stuffed peppers in a baking dish with a little coconut oil in the bottom of the dish. Put the pepper caps on top and bake for about 30 minutes, or until the peppers are tender.

Serves 6

Pan-Fried New York Strip Steak with Green Beans and Mixed Green Salad

....

Ingredients

    1 (10-ounce) New York strip steak

    2 teaspoons tamari (gluten-free soy sauce)

    ½ teaspoons garlic powder

    1½ teaspoons coconut oil

    8 ounces French cut green beans (haricot verts) lightly steamed

    1 cup raw mixed greens, such as green or red leaf lettuce

    Dressing, for serving (humans only)

For Canines: Before marinating the steak, cut off a raw section. For a small dog, cut off about 2 ounces; for a medium dog, cut off 3 ounces; for a large dog, cut off 6 ounces. Cut the raw steak into ½-inch cubes. Purée the lightly steamed green beans along with 1 cup of raw mixed greens (no dressing) in a food processor, using 2 to 3 ounces of green beans for small to medium dogs; 3 to 4 ounces for medium to large dogs. Mix the steak with the puréed greens and serve. Your dogs will love it.

For Humans Only: Poke holes in steak using a knife and place in a nonreactive bowl or a sealable plastic bag. Add the tamari and garlic powder and marinate for about 1 hour at room temperature.

Preheat the oven to 375 degrees.

Heat the oil in an ovenproof skillet over medium-high heat. When the coconut oil is hot, place the marinated steak in the skillet and pan-fry until the first side is nicely browned, about 8 minutes. Turn the steak over and transfer the skillet to the oven for about 8 minutes for medium rare. Remove the steak from the oven and let rest for a few minutes before serving.

Meanwhile, put green beans in a steamer and steam about 10 minutes. Serve the steak and green beans with the mixed green salad and your choice of dressing.

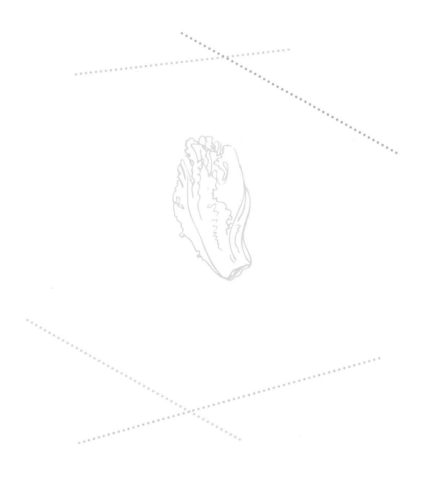

Gayle Pruitt

Lamb Entrées

Lamb Casserole

2 tablespoons oil

¼ teaspoon ground turmeric

½ teaspoon ground cumin

½ teaspoon ground coriander

1 teaspoon Celtic sea salt

1½ to 2 pounds boneless lamb shoulder, cut into 1-inch cubes

1 tablespoon coconut oil

1 small butternut squash, peeled and cut into 1-inch cubes

1 red bell pepper, seeded and cut into 1-inch squares

1 (15-ounce) can low-sodium, crushed tomatoes

Zest of 1 lemon, finely grated (about 1 teaspoon)

⅓ cup chicken broth (no onions)

½ cup dried figs

¼ bunch fresh flat-leaf parsley, finely chopped

Gluten-free noodles, for serving (optional)

In a large bowl, coat the lamb in the oil, spices, and salt, and refrigerate overnight.

In a large skillet over medium–high heat, warm the coconut oil. When the oil is hot, add the cubed lamb in small batches and brown. Transfer the browned meat to a 2-quart ceramic casserole dish. Add the squash, bell pepper, crushed tomatoes, lemon zest, broth, and figs to the casserole dish and bake for 2 hours, or until lamb is fork-tender. This is great served over gluten-free noodles.

Serves 6 to 8

Lamb Burgers with Cucumber Sauce

Burgers

1 pound ground lamb

1 tablespoon fresh flat-leaf parsley leaves, finely chopped (about ⅛ of a bunch)

1 teaspoon fresh mint leaves, finely chopped (4 or 5 fresh leaves)

½ teaspoon Celtic sea salt

½ teaspoons coconut oil

Sauce

1 pint Greek yogurt

2 medium cucumbers, peeled, seeded, and chopped

1 teaspoon fresh lemon juice

½ teaspoon finely grated lemon zest (optional)

Place all the ingredients for the burgers in a bowl and mix with your hands, then form into 4 patties.

Place a large skillet over medium-high heat. Add the coconut oil and, using a spatula, spread the oil over the bottom of the skillet. When the skillet is hot, add the patties and cook for about 8 minutes on one side. When each patty is brown, flip and cook on the opposite side for 5 minutes, or longer if needed.

Place all the sauce ingredients in a food processor and purée. Chill until needed.

Serve the patties with the yogurt-cucumber sauce.

Serves 4

Humans: Season to taste

Gayle Pruitt

Chicken
Entrées

Pumpkin Seed and Lime Chicken

Ingredients

    4 chicken quarters, bone in, skin on

    2 tablespoons olive oil

    2 ounces raw pumpkin seeds

    Juice and zest of 2 limes

    1 teaspoon ground turmeric

    ½ teaspoon Celtic sea salt

Add all the ingredients except for the chicken to a food processor and pulse until the pumpkin seeds are in small chunks. Put the chicken in a bowl and pour the pumpkin seed mixture over the chicken, making sure to completely cover it. Refrigerate for at least 1 hour.

Place the chicken, skin side down, in a hot skillet or grill pan. Place a cover over the top of the chicken, touching the chicken with the lid, and pressing down on the top of the chicken. Cook for about 10 minutes, then turn the chicken over; the skin should now be a golden brown. Reduce the heat to medium-low, re-place the lid over the chicken, and cook for another 30 minutes.

Serves 4 adult humans and 6 to 8 small to medium dogs

Oven-Fried Chicken

Ingredients

3 pounds chicken parts, bone in, skin on

2 cups goat milk kefir

1½ cups coconut flour

1 cup dried gluten-free bread crumbs (or make your own)

¼ cup melted coconut oil (or more if necessary)

2 teaspoons ground turmeric

2 teaspoons dried parsley

2 teaspoons Celtic sea salt

1 teaspoon mild paprika

Preheat the oven to 375 degrees. Apply a little melted coconut oil to a parchment paper–lined baking sheet or a grilling tray.

In a large bowl, combine the goat kefir and chicken parts and marinate in the refrigerator about 30 minutes, turning the chicken over several times, and making sure all the chicken parts are coated with the marinade. In a separate bowl mix together the flour, turmeric, parsley, paprika, and salt. Put the dried bread crumbs in another bowl. Working with 1 chicken piece at a time, coat the chicken with the flour mixture, then roll the chicken parts in the bread crumbs. Place the chicken on a platter, and let rest for 8 to 10 minutes.

Place the chicken on the lined baking sheet and drizzle the coconut oil over all the coated chicken pieces. Bake for 40 to 45 minutes until the chicken is cooked through and golden brown. To check for doneness, stick a fork in the chicken. The juices should run clear.

Serves 6

Cinnamon Chicken

Ingredients

    1 (2-pound) whole chicken

    2 unpeeled Granny Smith apples, seeded and cut into quarters

       (dogs should not consume apple seeds)

    1 teaspoon ground cinnamon

    ½ teaspoon mild paprika

    ½ cup chicken broth (no onions)

    Dash of Celtic sea salt

Preheat the oven to 350 degrees.

Put the apples and chicken in a 2-quart ceramic casserole dish. Add the chicken broth, then sprinkle the seasoning over the chicken and apples.

Bake for 45 minutes to 1 hour. The chicken meat should be coming off the bone. Serve with baked apples.

Serves 4

For dogs: Pull chicken meat off the bone and serve with the baked apples.

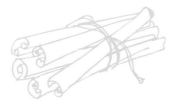

Chicken Pot Pie Cooked in Sweet Peppers

Gluten-free Pie crust

> ½ cup cold coconut oil, cut into 8 or 9 pieces and placed in freezer for about 5 minutes
>
> 2 cups gluten-free, all-purpose flour
>
> 1 teaspoon dried thyme
>
> 3 to 4 tablespoons ice water

Add the cold coconut oil pieces, flour, and dried thyme to a food processor. Pulse 5 or 6 times to cut the oil into the flour. Add the ice water, 1 tablespoon at a time while pulsing, being careful not to add too much water; the mixture should resemble small crumbs. Place the mixture in a plastic bag and form into a ball. Refrigerate the ball for at least 2 hours, or up to 2 days.

Filling

> 4 large bell peppers (any color)
>
> 2 tablespoons coconut oil
>
> 1½ tablespoons gluten-free, all-purpose flour
>
> Dash of Celtic sea salt
>
> 1 teaspoon dried thyme
>
> 4 medium carrots, peeled and diced
>
> 2 celery stalks, strings removed, diced
>
> 1 pint chicken broth (no onions)
>
> 1 chicken, poached, meat removed from the bones
>
> 1 teaspoon dried tarragon
>
> ½ cup frozen peas

Preheat the oven to 375 degrees.

Cut the tops off the bell peppers and remove the seeds and membranes. Steam the peppers for 6 to 7 minutes; they should still hold their shape.

Place the coconut oil, flour, salt, thyme, carrots, and celery in a skillet over medium-high heat. Reduce the heat to medium-low and cook for 2 to 3 minutes, being careful not to brown the flour.

Add the chicken broth and whisk until smooth. Cook until the mixture thickens, 4 to 5 minutes; it should coat the back of a spoon. Add the cooked chicken meat, tarragon, and peas and cook for 1 minute more.

Place the bell peppers in a greased, shallow rectangular glass baking dish and fill the peppers with the chicken and vegetable mixture, leaving about ½ inch of space at the top.

Roll out the pastry and cut to cover the top of the peppers. Cut a small crescent moon out of each top for venting steam. Bake the stuffed peppers for about 20 minutes.

Turn the oven to broil and broil the peppers for about 1 minute, or until the pastry top is golden brown. Serve immediately.

Serves 4 (You will have some filling leftovers.)

Black Rice Paella

Ingredients

3 tablespoons olive oil

1 tablespoon mild paprika

2 teaspoons dried oregano

1½ teaspoons ground turmeric

2 pounds boneless chicken thighs

1 teaspoon garlic powder

2 cups Forbidden Rice (black) or
  purple rice

Pinch of Spanish saffron

1 bay leaf

½ bunch flat-leaf parsley, finely chopped

1 quart chicken broth (no onions)

1 pound poached salmon

1 pint sugar snap peas, strings removed

2 roasted bell peppers, seeded and
  cut into strips (you may use jarred
  peppers)

In a medium bowl, mix together 1 tablespoon of the olive oil, the paprika, oregano, and turmeric. Coat the chicken thighs with the mixture and refrigerate for at least 1 hour or overnight.

Heat 1 tablespoon of the olive oil in a large skillet or paella pan over medium heat. Stir in the garlic powder and rice. Cook, stirring to coat rice with the oil, for about 3 minutes.

Stir in the saffron threads, bay leaf, parsley, and chicken broth and bring to a boil. Cover, reduce the heat to medium-low, and simmer for 20 minutes.

Meanwhile, heat the remaining 1 tablespoon olive oil in a separate skillet over medium heat. Add the chicken thighs, cover, and cook for about 20 minutes. Add the salmon and cook for about 8 minutes. Add peas and roasted red peppers and cook another 5 minutes. Remove and discard the bay leaf. Spread the rice mixture on a serving platter. Top with the chicken, salmon, roasted red peppers and peas.

Serves 15

Turkey
Entrées

Roast Turkey Breast

Ingredients

    2 tablespoons coconut oil

    1 tablespoon dried rubbed sage

    Pinch of Celtic sea salt

    1 cup turkey or chicken broth (no onions)

    1 (5½- to 6-pound) turkey breast, bone-in

Preheat the oven to 325 degrees.

Combine the soft coconut oil with the sage and salt and mix well to form a paste. Loosen the turkey skin with your fingers and gently push part of the coconut mixture under the turkey breast skin. Rub the rest on top of the skin.

Pour the chicken broth into a roasting pan. Place the turkey breast, skin side up, on a rack in the roasting pan and place in the oven. Roast the turkey for 1½ to 2¼ hours until the skin is golden brown and an instant-read thermometer registers 165° F when inserted into the thickest and meatiest areas of the breast. (I test in several places.)

If the skin is browning too quickly, cover the breast loosely with aluminum foil. When the turkey is done, cover with foil and allow it to rest at room temperature for 15 to 20 minutes before slicing. Slice and serve with the pan juices spooned over the turkey.

Serves 10

Turkey Tetrazzini

Ingredients

- 7 ounces dried brown rice fettuccine
- 1 tablespoon coconut oil (or butter)
- 1 tablespoon gluten-free, all-purpose flour
- 1 cup turkey broth
- 2 cups cubed cooked turkey
- ½ red bell pepper, seeded and cut into small dice
- ½ cup frozen green peas
- 2 tablespoons finely chopped celery
- 3 ounces green beans, cut into 1-inch pieces

Topping

- ¼ cup dried Udi's gluten-free bread crumbs (or make your own bread crumbs)
- 1½ teaspoons coconut oil (or butter)

Preheat the oven to 350 degrees.

Cook the fettuccine until almost done.

Place a tablespoon of coconut oil in a saucepan over medium heat. Add the gluten-free flour and cook for about 1 minute, or until the roux starts to bubble. Add the turkey broth all at once, whisk, and cook until the mixture thickens.

In a large bowl, combine the turkey, bell pepper, peas, celery, green beans, fettuccine, and thickened sauce and stir together gently.

Smear a small amount of coconut oil in a 2-quart baking dish, covering bottom and sides. Pour the turkey mixture into the greased baking dish.

In a small bowl, combine the topping ingredients and mix thoroughly. Sprinkle over the turkey mixture. Cover the dish and bake for 30 minutes, or until it starts to bubble. Uncover and bake another 5 to 10 minutes until topping is a golden brown.

Serves 4

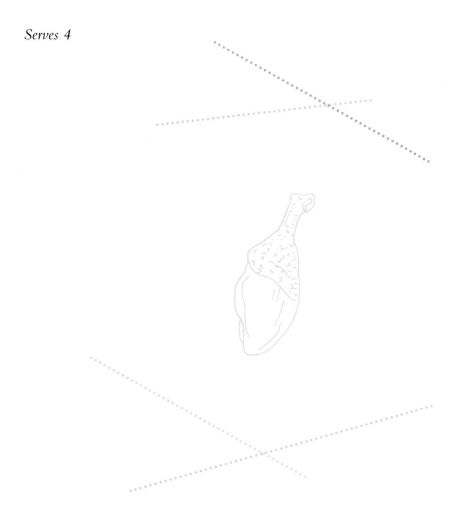

Old-Time Turkey à la King

Ingredients

    ¼ cup coconut oil

    ½ cup green bell peppers, seeded and finely chopped

    ½ cup red bell pepper, seeded and finely chopped (or a jar of pimiento strips)

    ¼ cup gluten-free, all-purpose flour

    1½ cups turkey or chicken broth (no onions)

    3 cups cooked, cubed turkey

Melt the coconut oil in a large skillet over medium heat. Add the bell peppers, cover, and cook for 5 minutes. Remove the vegetables from the skillet.

Add the flour to the coconut oil in the skillet and stir until smooth. Add the broth and cook until thickened. Add the cubed turkey and peppers.

Serve with brown rice, brown rice noodles, or toasted gluten-free bread.

For humans: Add your favorite seasonings.

Serves 6

Turkey Meatballs

Ingredients

    1 pound ground turkey

    ½ cup cooked brown rice

    1 large egg or 2 small eggs

    ½ green bell pepper, seeded and cut into small dice

    Pinch of fennel seeds

    Pinch of dried oregano

    Dash of Celtic sea salt

    1 tablespoon coconut oil, melted

    1 (15-ounce) can low-sodium organic tomato sauce

Preheat the oven to 325 degrees.

Mix all the ingredients except for the coconut oil and tomato sauce together in a bowl and form into 1-inch balls. Place the meatballs in a glass or ceramic baking dish. Drizzle the melted coconut oil and the tomato sauce over the meatballs. Bake for 30 minutes, or until done.

Serves 6

Turkey Curry

Ingredients

 2 tablespoons coconut oil

 1 teaspoon fenugreek seeds, ground

 1 teaspoon ground turmeric

 1 tablespoon gluten-free, all-purpose flour

 ½ teaspoon ground ginger

 1 cup chicken broth

 4 ounces cubed fresh pineapple

 2 cups diced cooked turkey

Heat the coconut oil in a large skillet over medium heat. Add the ground fenugreek seed and turmeric, stir, and cook for 2 minutes. Blend in the gluten-free flour and ginger. Add the chicken broth and pineapple. Cook for about 5 minutes. Stir in the turkey and cook for another 8 minutes.

Serve with brown rice.

Serves 4

      Gayle Pruitt

Turkey Salad–Two Ways

Here are two delicious recipes for leftover turkey.

Ingredients

    1 pound cooked turkey meat, cubed

    2 celery stalks, coarsely chopped

    ½ red bell pepper, seeded and coarsely chopped

    3 tablespoons mayonnaise

    1 teaspoon apple cider vinegar

Turkey Salad #1 : Mix all the ingredients together and refrigerate for 2 hours. Serve with mixed salad greens. Purée the greens for canines.

Turkey Salad #2 : Place all the ingredients in food processor and process until smooth. Refrigerate overnight. To serve, spread on rounds of zucchini or crook-neck squash.

Fish
Entrées

Whole Redfish

Ingredients

    1 tablespoon tamari sauce (Normally I wouldn't suggest a soy product but
       tamari is fermented soy. Always purchase gluten-free.)

    1 tablespoon coconut oil

    1 lemon, cut into 6 slices

    1½ pounds whole redfish

    7 to 8 fresh basil leaves

    Fresh basil, for garnish (optional)

Have the fish market clean and scale the fish.

In a large skillet over medium-high heat combine the soy, oil, and lemon slices. Cook for about 2 minutes.

Stuff the basil leaves into the cavity of the fish. Place the fish in the skillet, cover, and reduce the heat to medium-low. Cook approximately 10 minutes. Check for doneness: Using a knife, pull the flesh from the bone; the flesh should resist slightly pulling away from the bone.

Remove the skillet from the heat. The fish will continue cooking for a minute or so.

Transfer the fish gently to a platter and arrange the caramelized lemon slices around the fish. Garnish the platter with more basil, if using. Serve immediately.

Serves 6

Salmon Florentine

Ingredients

¼ of a 16-ounce bag frozen spinach, thawed, drained, and squeezed of excess moisture

¼ of a 15-ounce carton ricotta cheese

1 tablespoon grated Parmesan cheese

1 large egg

1 tablespoon olive oil

2 cups cooked rice

2 tablespoons chicken broth (no onions)

2 (6-ounce) salmon fillets

Lemon slices, for garnish

Preheat the oven to 350 degrees.

Add the spinach, ricotta, grated cheese, and egg to a food processor and purée.

Brush the oil on the bottom and sides of a glass, ovenproof dish. Add the rice to the bottom of the dish and spread out evenly. Spoon the chicken broth evenly over the rice.

Place the salmon fillets over the rice and spoon the spinach mixture over the top.

Bake for about 20 minutes; when done, the spinach should be puffed.

Garnish with lemon slices.

Serves 2

Salmon Asparagus Salad with Seaweed Noodles

....

Ingredients

    1 handful mixed salad greens such as baby arugula and spinach

    1 bunch asparagus, lightly steamed

    1 (8-ounce) package seaweed (kelp) noodles, uncooked

    1 (8-ounce) package smoked sliced salmon or poached salmon

Place the mixed salad greens on a large platter. Arrange the steamed asparagus over the greens. Put the uncooked seaweed noodles in the middle of the greens and asparagus.

Cut the salmon into 1-inch strips and drape over the greens and asparagus on the platter.

For Humans: Dress with your favorite dressing.

For Canines: Purée in a food processor.

Serves 4

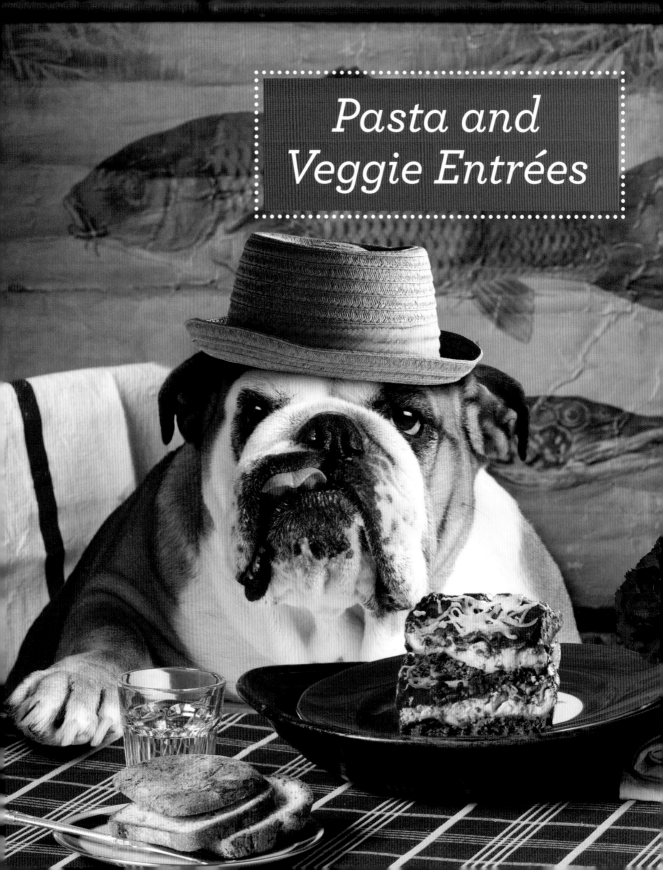

Pasta and Veggie Entrées

Individual Spinach-Kale Lasagnas

Ingredients

    1 bunch kale, stemmed

    ½ (16-ounce) bag frozen spinach, thawed, drained (squeezed of
        excess moisture)

    1 (15-ounce) container ricotta cheese

    1 pasture-raised egg

    1 tablespoon dried oregano

    1 teaspoon Celtic sea salt

    2 tablespoons olive oil

    1 (15-ounce) can organic crushed tomatoes

    12-inch, no-boil, brown rice lasagna noodles

    Shredded mozzarella; enough to cover 6 mini lasagnas (Leave this off your
        canine pals' version.)

Preheat the oven to 350 degrees.

Add the kale, spinach, ricotta, egg, oregano, and salt to a food processor and process until fairly smooth.

Brush the inside of 8 mini loaf pans with olive oil. Spoon a tablespoon of the crushed tomatoes into the bottom of each pan.

Place the lasagna noodles in boiling water for about 4 minutes. (You can leave this step out, but the lasagna cuts better if you boil it for 4 minutes). Cut the partially cooked noodles into 12 pieces to fit the mini loaf pans; place one on the bottom of each pan. Add enough crushed tomatoes to cover the noodles.

Spoon the spinach-kale mixture to almost fill each mini pan by three-quarters. Place lasagna noodles over the top of each mini loaf and cover with more tomato sauce.

For humans only: Sprinkle the mozzarella over the top. You can stack lasagnas for the big guys.

Bake for 25 minutes. Remove from oven and let rest for 10 minutes. (Cool for dogs; it should be warm to touch, but not hot).

Serve on plates with salad.

Purée salad greens before serving them to your furry buddies.

Serves 8

Gayle Pruitt

Manicotti

Crepe

- 1 cup gluten-free, all-purpose flour
- 1 cup, plus 1 tablespoon water or other liquid
- 2 large eggs
- ½ teaspoon Celtic sea salt
- 1 tablespoon melted coconut oil

Whisk together the flour, 1 cup of the water, the eggs, and salt. The batter should be very thin and just coat the back of a spoon.

Heat a nonstick 8-inch crepe pan or a small skillet over medium heat and brush the pan with melted oil. Add ⅓ cup of the batter, and swirl to spread the mixture over the surface, making a circle about 4 inches in diameter. Cook for about 2 minutes, or until the sides turn a light brown. Loosen the crepe with a spatula, flip it, and cook on the opposite side for about 30 seconds. Continue to make crepes with the remaining batter; you will need a total of 6.

Filling

- 1 (28-ounce) can organic diced tomatoes
- 1 teaspoon dried oregano
- ½ teaspoon garlic powder (optional)
- 1 (15-ounce) carton ricotta cheese
- 1 large egg
- ½ pound cooked turkey, chopped
- ¼ cup grated Parmesan cheese
- 4 ounces sliced mozzarella cheese

Preheat the oven to 350 degrees.

Add 4 ounces of the tomatoes, the oregano, garlic powder, ricotta cheese, and egg to a food processer and process for about 1 minute. Pour into a large bowl. Stir in the chopped cooked turkey.

Into a shallow, rectangular glass ovenproof dish, pour 1 cup of the remaining tomatoes covering the bottom of the dish.

Spoon about 2 ounces of the turkey-cheese mixture into each crepe and roll up. Place each of them into the dish, seam side down, on the tomatoes. Pour the remaining tomatoes over the stuffed manicotti and sprinkle with the Parmesan cheese. Cover the dish and bake for about 15 minutes.

For humans only: Remove the dish from the oven, remove the cover, and place the sliced mozzarella over the manicotti. Return the dish to the oven and bake for about 5 minutes or until the cheese has melted.

Serve immediately.

Serves 8

Twice-Baked Broccoli Asparagus Soufflés

*This recipe was inspired by Cooking with Barry & Meta at
www.cookingwithbarryandmeta.blogspot.com. They posted a
Twice-Baked Green Onion Soufflé; this is my dairy- and gluten-free version.*

Ingredients

6 tablespoons olive oil

⅓ cup Udi's gluten-free bread, dried, processed into bread crumbs

1 cup broccoli, chopped

½ cup asparagus, chopped

3 tablespoons gluten-free, all-purpose flour

1 cup carrot juice

1 teaspoon olive oil

½ teaspoon Celtic sea salt

5 large eggs, separated

½ teaspoon cream of tartar

Preheat the oven to 350 degrees F.

Place eight 8- to 10-ounce ramekins or custard cups (¾ cup capacity) in a shallow roasting or broiler pan. Brush the insides of the ramekins with olive oil, using 1 to 2 tablespoons total, then sprinkle with the bread crumbs.

Add the chopped broccoli, asparagus, and remaining 4 tablespoons olive oil to a saucepan over medium-high heat and sauté for 3 to 4 minutes. Reduce the heat to low and cook for 2 minutes more, stirring constantly.

Add the flour and cook for 2 minutes, whisking constantly. Gradually whisk in the carrot juice. Increase the heat to medium and cook for 5 minutes, or until the sauce comes to a boil and thickens, whisking constantly and adjusting the heat if necessary. Whisk in the salt. Let cool slightly.

Whisk egg yolks in large bowl until combined, then gradually stir them into the hot mixture until blended.

Beat the egg whites and the cream of tartar in a large mixer bowl on low speed until foamy. Increase the speed to medium and beat until slightly firm, but not stiff, peaks form.

Fold one-third of the egg whites into broccoli-asparagus mixture until almost blended. Gently fold in an additional one-third, and then the remaining egg whites.

Spoon the mixture into the ramekins; the mixture will come almost to the top. Run the tip of a small knife through the soufflé mixture ½ inch from the edge to help the soufflés rise evenly. Add enough boiling water to the roasting pan to come almost halfway up the sides of the ramekins.

Bake for 25 to 30 minutes until the soufflés are puffed and browned. Remove the roasting pan from the oven, and let the ramekins stand in the water for 10 minutes after baking.

Remove the ramekins from the water.

Place on a wire rack, and let stand for 30 minutes, or until cool enough to handle.[*]

Meanwhile, lightly spray a small rimmed baking sheet with cooking spray. Run the tip of a small knife or thin spatula around the inside edge of the ramekins and gently turn out the soufflés. Place, topside up, on baking sheet.

Cover and refrigerate overnight, or until ready to reheat. The soufflés can be made up to this point 1 day ahead. In this case, to serve, preheat the oven to 400 degrees. Place the room-temperature soufflés into the oven and reheat for 10 minutes, or until the soufflés are slightly puffed and hot. Serve immediately.

Makes 8 individual soufflés

* The soufflés can be served immediately in the ramekins, if desired.

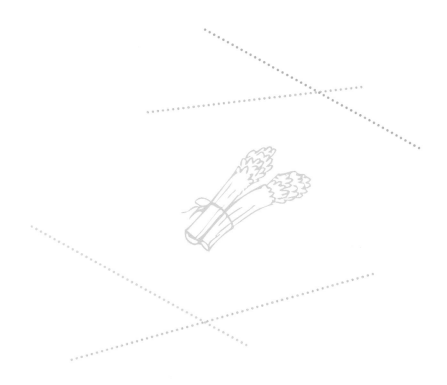

Sides

When enjoying a meal with friends, human or canine, it's lovely to serve delicious side dishes that enhance that great entrée you are serving.

The side dishes in this section are some of Mimi's, Mister Casper's, and my favorites. We hope you enjoy them, too.

Baked Beets

Ingredients

   1 pound beets, trimmed and stemmed

   1 tablespoon melted coconut oil

Preheat the oven to 375 degrees.

Place the coconut oil and beets in a glass or ceramic casserole dish, cover, and bake for about 1 hour, or until fork-tender. Remove the skins.

You may eat the beets hot or cool, or slice to be used in salads.

Serves 6

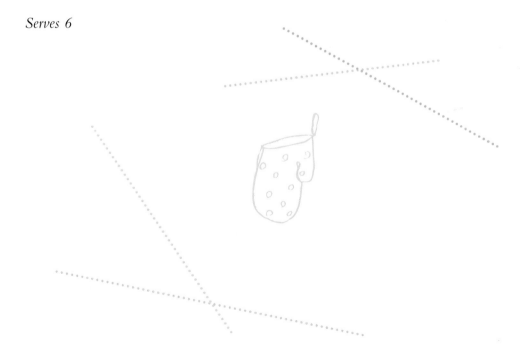

Beets in Ginger

Ingredients

    1 pound beets, baked (see recipe for Baked Beets page 107)

    1 tablespoon coconut oil

    1½ teaspoons peeled and grated fresh ginger

    1½ teaspoons balsamic or apple cider vinegar

Slice the baked beets into rounds.

In a skillet over medium-high heat, warm the coconut oil. Add the ginger and beets and cook for about 3 minutes.

Toss with the vinegar.

Serves 6

Beets with Cranberry and Cloves in Honey Sauce

Ingredients

    1 tablespoon butter

    ½ teaspoon ground cloves

    1 teaspoon fresh lemon juice

    ½ cup puréed fresh or frozen cranberries

    1 tablespoon honey (Humans only: you may substitute Stevia)

    1 pound baked beets, sliced (see Baked Beets page 107)

Melt the butter in a skillet over medium-low heat. Add the ground cloves, lemon juice, puréed cranberries, and honey, stir, and cook for about 1 minute.

Add the beets, stir, and cook until the beets are heated through.

Serves 6

Baked Cauliflower

Ingredients

    1 large head cauliflower

    ½ cup seasoned gluten-free bread crumbs

    1 tablespoon grated Parmesan cheese

    ¼ cup coconut oil, melted

    ⅛ teaspoon garlic powder (optional)

    ⅛ teaspoon Celtic sea salt

    Pinch of dried oregano

    1 cup chicken broth (no onions)

Preheat the oven to 375 degrees.

Steam a whole head of cauliflower for about 20 minutes, or until tender.

In a medium bowl, mix together the bread crumbs, grated cheese, and melted coconut oil. Season with garlic powder, salt, and oregano and mix well.

Add the chicken broth to a glass or ceramic baking dish. Place the head of cauliflower in the dish and coat with the bread-crumb mixture.

Bake until golden brown, 10 to 15 minutes.

Serves 6 to 8

Caramelized Acorn Squash with Roasted Red Peppers and Brussels Sprouts

....

Ingredients

   3 tablespoons butter

   2 large acorn squash, cut in half, pulp removed

   1 branch Brussels sprouts (about 20 small sprouts)

   2 red bell peppers, roasted (you may use roasted jarred peppers)

Preheat the oven to 350 degrees.

Melt 2 tablespoons of the butter and pour into a large, rectangular glass baking dish.

Place the squash cut side down in the dish and bake for about 35 minutes. Check to see if the squash has caramelized, if not, continue to bake for another 10 minutes.

Lightly steam the whole Brussels sprouts; cut them in half when done.

Place the remaining 1 tablespoon butter in a skillet over medium-high heat. Add the Brussels sprouts and sauté until browned. Add the roasted red peppers and heat through.

Remove the caramelized squash from the oven and fill each cavity with the Brussels sprouts and bell peppers.

Serves 6 to 8

Caramelized Carrots and Zucchini

Ingredients
- 2 pats butter
- ½ pound carrots, peeled and julienned
- 3 small zucchini, julienned

In a skillet over medium-high heat, melt the butter. Add the carrots, stir, and cook until they take on a reddish-brown color, 8 to 10 minutes.

Add the zucchini and cook for another 3 to 4 minutes.

Carrots and Zucchini with Tarragon

Ingredients
- 1 tablespoon butter or coconut oil
- 3 medium carrots, washed, peeled, and sliced into thin carrot sticks (save the peelings for bulk dog food recipes)
- 2 zucchini, washed and cut into ¼-inch-thick sticks
- 1 teaspoon dried tarragon

Melt the butter or coconut oil in a skillet over medium-high heat. Add the carrots and cook for about 1 minute. Add the zucchini and cook for 1 minute. Remove the vegetables from the skillet, sprinkle with tarragon, and serve.

Serves about 4

Celery Root and Cauliflower Mash

Ingredients

    2 celery roots (celeriac), peeled and chopped

    1 cauliflower, separated into florets

    2 cups vegetable or chicken broth (no onions)

Add the vegetables and broth to a large pot and cook for about 15 minutes, or until the vegetables are very tender.

Drain the vegetables and mash with a potato masher.

For humans only: You may stir in a little butter and season to taste with salt and pepper.

Serves 6

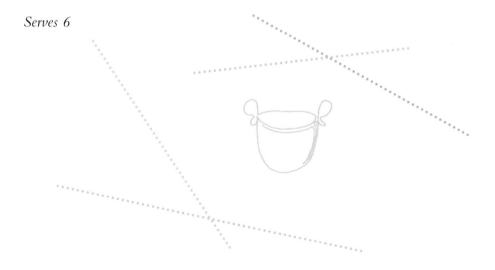

Fennel and Brussels Sprouts

Ingredients

    1 teaspoon whole fennel seeds

    1 tablespoon unsalted butter

    2 fennel bulbs, trimmed and chopped

    10 medium Brussels sprouts, finely chopped

    8 or 9 whole almonds, sliced

Crush the fennel seeds with a mortar and pestle.

Melt the butter in a skillet over medium-high heat. Add the chopped fennel, Brussels sprouts, and ground fennel seeds and cook for about 10 minutes, or until the vegetables are tender.

Add the sliced almonds and cook for 1 minute more.

Serves 4

For humans only: Adding 1 ounce of ouzo, the aperitif of Greece, to this side dish is really delicious.

Roasted Carrots and Peas

Ingredients

    1 pound medium carrots, peeled and sliced lengthwise

    1 tablespoon butter

    ½ teaspoon dried tarragon

    1 (10-ounce) package frozen peas

Put the carrots, butter, and tarragon in a glass or ceramic casserole dish and bake for 35 minutes, or until tender.

Add the frozen peas and cook for 5 minutes more.

Serves 6

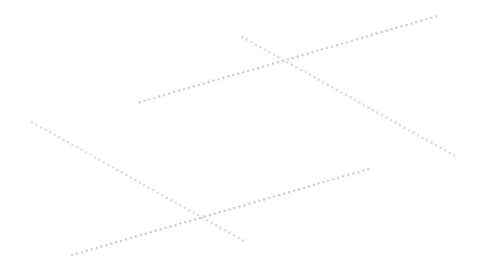

Gayle Pruitt

Roasted Root Vegetables

Ingredients

    1 pound medium carrots, peeled

    2 whole medium beets, cleaned

    1 rutabaga, peeled and quartered

    1 sweet potato, quartered

    2 tablespoons olive oil

Preheat the oven to 350 degrees.

Place all the vegetables and oil in a large glass or ceramic casserole dish, cover, and bake for 90 minutes, or until the vegetables are tender.

Serves 6

Humans: Season with salt and pepper, to taste.

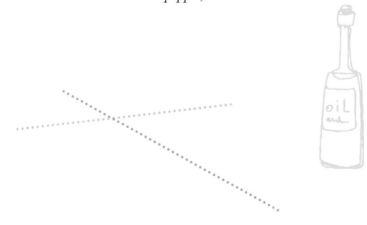

Spinach and Yellow Bell Pepper

Ingredients

    1 tablespoon butter

    2 bunches spinach, cleaned, stemmed, and chopped

    1 medium yellow pepper, seeded and julienned

    2 tablespoons chicken or vegetable broth (no onion)

In a hot skillet over medium-high heat, melt the butter. Add the chopped spinach and julienned yellow pepper and sauté for about 3 minutes.

Add the broth and cook for about 2 minutes more.

Serves 4

Gayle Pruitt

Sugar Snap Peas with Sesame Seeds

Ingredients

    1 pound sugar snap peas, strings removed

    1 tablespoon raw sesame seeds

    1 teaspoon sesame oil

Fill a bowl with ice and water. Set aside.

Blanch the peas in boiling water for about 3 minutes; then shock in ice water.

In a hot dry skillet, toast the sesame seeds for 1 minute.

In a bowl, stir together the peas, oil, and toasted sesame seeds to combine. Serve.

Serves 6

Summer Squash with Cilantro and Parsley

....

My friend Millie introduced me to cilantro and summer squash and I love it!

Ingredients

    1 tablespoon extra-virgin olive oil

    1 pound yellow crookneck squash, cut into ½-inch rounds

    2 tablespoons fresh cilantro, finely chopped

    1 tablespoon fresh parsley, finely chopped

Warm the oil in a skillet over medium-low heat. Add the squash and sauté for about 5 minutes.

Add the cilantro and cook for 1 minute more.

Sprinkle with the parsley just before serving.

Serves 4

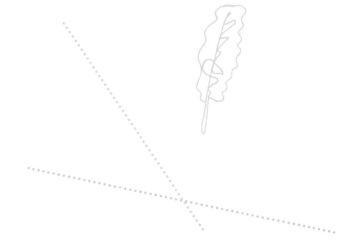

Fettuccine with Yellow Squash and Snow Peas

Ingredients

   1 pound brown rice fettuccine

   20 snow peas, strings removed

   2 small or 1 medium yellow crookneck squash, cut into rounds

   ¼ cup fresh cilantro, chopped

   1 tablespoon extra-virgin olive oil

   1 teaspoon apple cider vinegar

Cook the fettuccine in a large pot of boiling water for 9 minutes.

Add the snow peas and squash and cook for 1 minute more, then drain.

In a large bowl, combine the pasta, peas, squash, cilantro, oil, and vinegar and mix gently. Serve warm or chilled.

For dogs: Place a small amount over their food.

For humans: Season to taste.

Serves 4

Quinoa with Carrots and Kale

Ingredients

    1 tablespoon extra-virgin olive oil

    1 cup quinoa

    2⅛ cups water, beef, chicken, or vegetable broth (no onion)

    2 medium carrots, peeled and sliced into small coins

    ½ bunch kale, chopped

In a saucepan over medium-high heat, combine the olive oil, quinoa, carrots, and liquid. Let the liquid come to a boil; then reduce the heat to medium-low, cover, and cook for 15 minutes.

Add the chopped kale, cover, and cook for 10 minutes more.

Remove from the heat and let sit for 5 minutes. Uncover and fluff the quinoa and vegetables with a fork.

Humans: Season to taste.

Serves 4

Turkey and Quinoa Dressing

Ingredients

    1 cup quinoa

    1½ teaspoons coconut oil

    2 celery stalks, chopped

    2 bay leaves

    1 teaspoon dried rubbed sage

    2 cups turkey broth

    1 cup diced cooked turkey

Combine the coconut oil and quinoa in a skillet over medium-high heat, stir, and cook for 2 minutes.

Add the remaining ingredients and bring to a gentle boil. Reduce the heat to medium-low, cover, and simmer for 25 minutes. Remove from the heat and let sit for 5 minutes. Remove and discard the bay leaves.

Serves 4

Millet-Cranberry Dressing

Ingredients

    1 rounded tablespoon coconut oil

    1 cup millet

    2 bell peppers (1 green, 1 red), seeded and coarsely chopped

    2 celery stalks, strings removed, finely chopped

    2½ cups chicken broth (no onions)

    2 teaspoons dried rubbed sage

    ¾ cup fresh or frozen cranberries

    Fresh sage, for garnish

    Celtic sea salt to human taste

In a large skillet or stockpot over medium-high heat, warm the coconut oil. Add the millet, bell peppers, and celery and sauté for 2 to 3 minutes.

Add 2 cups of the chicken broth and the dried rubbed sage and cranberries. Reduce the heat to medium-low, cover, and simmer for about 40 minutes.

After 40 minutes, check to see if liquid has been absorbed. If so, add the remaining ½ cup chicken broth and cook for another 20 minutes; the dressing should be moist but not soupy. Season with salt to taste; do not add salt to canine portions.

Garnish with fresh sage leaves and serve with roast turkey breast.

Serves 4

Yellow Rice

....

I make a large batch of rice and freeze it in individual packages.

Ingredients

   3 cups short-grain brown rice

   2 tablespoons coconut oil

   1 tablespoon ground turmeric

   1 teaspoon mild paprika

   4 to 5 bay leaves

   ½ teaspoon Celtic sea salt

   7 cups water or beef or chicken broth (no onion)

In a large skillet over medium-high heat, combine the rice, coconut oil, turmeric, paprika, bay leaves and salt and sauté for about 2 minutes. Add the liquid, cover, and reduce the heat to low. Cook for 60 minutes, or until done. Remove and discard the bay leaves.

Serves 12 to 15

Brown Rice Pilaf with Slivered Almonds, Red Peppers, and Snap Peas

Ingredients

2 teaspoons extra-virgin olive oil

1 cup long grain brown rice

2½ cups chicken broth or water

½ cup slivered almonds

1 red bell pepper, seeded and cut into small squares

15 sugar snap peas, strings removed

Combine the oil and rice in saucepan over medium-high heat and stir to coat each rice grain with the oil.

Add the liquid and almonds and bring to a boil. Reduce the heat to low, cover, and cook for 30 minutes.

Add the bell peppers, cover, and cook for 10 minutes more. Remove from the heat and add the peas. Let rest, covered, for 5 minutes. Fluff with a fork and serve.

Serves 4

Cherry Tomatoes and Black or Purple Rice

....

Ingredients

1 tablespoon olive oil

1 cup black or purple rice

1 yellow bell pepper, seeded and
  chopped

1 teaspoon peeled and minced
  fresh ginger

½ teaspoon ground fenugreek

½ teaspoon ground turmeric

2 cups water

2 cups cherry tomatoes, halved

¼ cup finely chopped fresh parsley

2 tablespoons finely chopped fresh
  cilantro

In a saucepan over medium heat, combine the oil, rice, bell pepper, ginger, fenu-greek, and turmeric. Stir for 2 to 3 minutes, making sure all the grains have been coated with oil.

Add the water, cover, and cook for about 10 minutes. Reduce the heat to low and cook for 15 minutes more or until all the water has been absorbed. Remove from the heat and let sit, covered, for about 10 minutes.

Stir in the tomatoes, parsley, and cilantro and serve.

For Humans: Season to taste

For Canines: Spoon over a meat dish or their normal bulk food.

Serves 4

Dirty Dog Rice

Ingredients

    6 cups chicken broth (no onions)

    1 pound beef hearts, chopped

    1 pound chicken or beef livers, chopped

    Salt

    1 tablespoon Worcestershire sauce

    ½ teaspoon mild paprika, or to taste

    3 tablespoons olive oil

    1 large green bell pepper, seeded and chopped

    1 large red bell pepper, seeded and chopped

    3 celery stalks, strings removed, coarsely chopped

    1 pound ground beef (labled 90 percent lean)

    2½ cups long-grain brown rice

    1 cup parsley, chopped

Heat the chicken stock in a 12-quart stockpot and add the hearts and livers, along with the salt, Worcestershire sauce, and paprika. Cover and gently simmer for 15 minutes.

In a large skillet over medium-low heat, warm the oil. Add the peppers and celery and sauté until tender. Remove from the skillet and transfer to a bowl.

Add the ground beef to the skillet and sauté until lightly browned. Drain the meat in a colander and discard the fat.

Remove the livers and hearts from the chicken broth, and reserve the stock.

When cool, place the livers and heart in a food processor and pulse for about 1 minute.

Add the liver and heart mixture, along with the browned meats, to the vegetables. Transfer all to the stockpot and add ½ cup of the reserved chicken broth. Cover and simmer for 15 to 20 minutes.

Cook the rice, using the reserved chicken stock. Add the cooked rice to the vegetables and meat and gently stir in the parsley.

Serves 10 to 15 humans

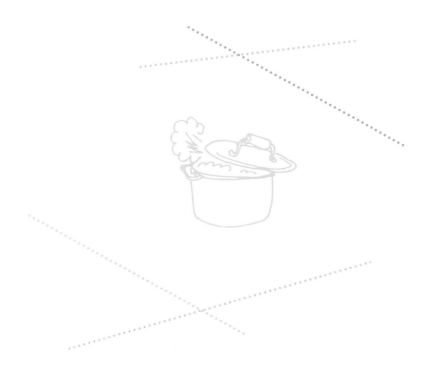

Desserts

Coconut Chia Pudding with Blueberries

Ingredients

    2 cups unsweetened coconut milk

    2 tablespoons unsweetened shredded coconut

    4 teaspoons chia seeds

    ½ teaspoon ground cinnamon

    1 cup fresh, organic blueberries

Mix all the ingredients together in a bowl. Cover and let macerate overnight in the refrigerator. Serve with the blueberries.

Humans only: You may add stevia as a sweetener.

Serves 4

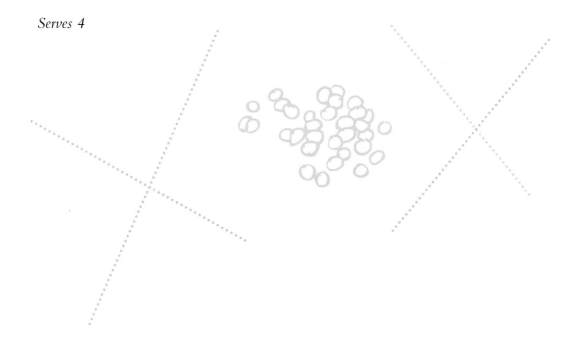

Pears with Raspberry Sauce

Ingredients

  2 Bosc pears, peeled

  2 cups unsweetened cranberry juice

  1 stick cinnamon

  2 cups fresh or frozen raspberries

  1 cup mascarpone cheese, whipped

  ¼ cup stevia (optional: for humans only)

  Fresh mint leaves, for garnish

In a saucepan, poach the peeled pears in cranberry juice with the cinnamon stick for about 20 minutes. Remove from the heat and let cool. Transfer the cooled pears and liquid to a plastic bag and refrigerate overnight, turning once. Add stevia for humans, not for dogs.

Purée the raspberries, reserving 8 or 9 whole.

Cut the pears in half and remove the cores and seeds.

Put the whipped cheese in a plastic bag with a small hole cut at one corner and squeeze the cheese into dessert dish (or dog dish). Place a pear half over the cheese and pour the raspberry purée over the pear and cheese. Garnish with the whole raspberries and mint leaves.

Mini Fruit Tarts

Almond Pastry

    1¾ cups almond meal

    3 tablespoons cold coconut oil, plus 1 tablespoon, if needed

    2 tablespoons shredded unsweetened coconut

Preheat the oven to 375 degrees.

Put the almond meal and shredded coconut in a large bowl. Add the cold coconut oil and, using a pastry cutter, cut the coconut oil into the almond meal until the mixture resembles coarse crumbs. If the almond meal is very dry, add a little more coconut oil as needed.

Add 1 rounded tablespoon of the almond mixture to the bottom of each cup of a 24-cup mini muffin pan and, using your fingers, press the mixture onto the bottom and up the sides of the cups. Chill for 10 to 15 minutes.

Bake for about 10 minutes, or until the crusts are a light golden brown. Remove from the oven and cool. Unmold the tart shells carefully.

Filling

    8 ounces mascarpone cheese

    4 ounces frozen strawberries, thawed

    8 ounces fresh blueberries

    8 ounces fresh strawberries (cut in a fanlike shape if desired) (optional)

Combine the mascarpone cheese and the thawed strawberries and mix well. Fill the tart shells with the cheese and strawberry mixture. Then top the tarts with the blueberries or the strawberries or a mixture of both.

Humans only: Add 1 tablespoon of stevia to the cheese and strawberry mixture and sprinkle a little stevia on top of fresh fruit.

Makes 48 mini muffins

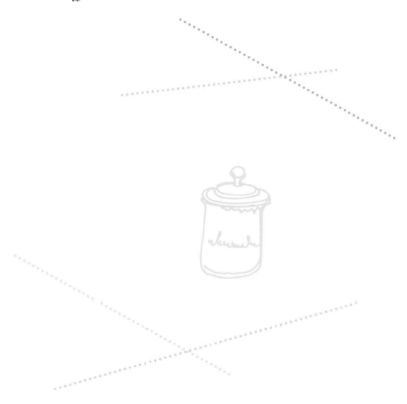

Minty Fruit Roll-Ups

2 cups organic raspberries

2 cups blackberries

1 tablespoon fresh spearmint leaves (8 or 9 leaves), chopped

¼ teaspoon fresh ginger, peeled and minced

¼ teaspoon ground turmeric

1 teaspoon any oil (optional)

Turn the oven on to the lowest temperature. If the lowest temperature in your oven is 170 degrees, then leave the oven door slightly ajar.

Place all the ingredients except for the oil in a food processer and purée. Put a little oil on baking sheet and cut parchment paper to fit baking sheet: The oil will keep the parchment paper smooth. You may also use a nonstick baking mat for better results. Spread the fruit purée thinly onto the lined baking sheet and put in the oven to dry. It should take 6 to 8 hours.

If you use a dehydrator, it will take a few hours longer to dry, due to the lower temperature, but it is well worth it.

When the fruit leather is dry, you can use a pizza cutter or scissors to cut it into strips about 1½ inches wide. Roll the dried fruit purée up while still slightly warm and store in the refrigerator.

Serves 4

Raspberry-Strawberry Kefir Drink

Ingredients

    1 cup plain goat milk kefir

    ½ cup fresh or frozen raspberries

    ½ cup fresh or frozen strawberries

    ¼ banana

    Sprig of fresh mint (humans only)

Place all the ingredients in a blender and blend until smooth. For humans, you may add a sprig of fresh mint. *This is delicious!*

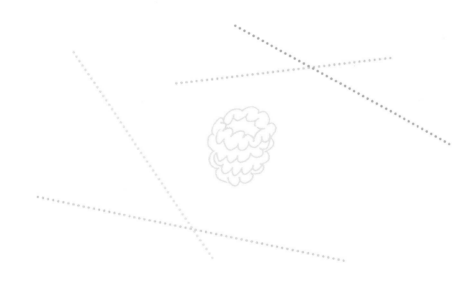

Juices

Juicing for your DOG? What has the world come to? Perhaps a little more understanding about what keeps humans and canines healthy.

Inexpensive juicers can be found almost anywhere. They are simple to use and easy to clean. Just put the veggies and fruits down the chute and catch the juice in a bowl or small pitcher.

Fresh juice tastes great, and juicing gives us vitamins and minerals in more abundance, helps cleanse our bodies of free radicals, improves our immune system, our eyesight, our memory, and so much more. And, no surprise, it can do the same for your dog.

Don't throw away the pulp after you finish juicing. Take the leftover fiber and freeze it to use in bulk dog food, which adds fiber and some antioxidants. It's easy, and so much healthier than most commercial dog food ingredients.

The juices below are easy recipes; no need for expensive exotic foods—just everyday fare—yet so fresh and delicious. You and your darling mutts will feel the difference in your energy levels.

One more little thing I do with Mimi and Casper: We use a supplement called Cell Food in our juices. It's a little expensive but well worth it and it lasts a long time. This product adds more oxygen to your cells while it helps eliminate free radicals.

Okay, now give juicing a try!

JUICE 1: GREAT FOR DIGESTION

    2 medium cucumbers, peeled
    2 celery stalks
    1 (¼-inch piece) fresh ginger
    ½ unpeeled Granny Smith Apple, seeds removed

JUICE 2: GOOD FOR IMMUNE SYSTEM, WATER RETENTION, AND EYESIGHT

2 asparagus spears

2 medium carrots

3 celery stalks

JUICE 3: GREAT CLEANSER

2 celery stalks

⅛ bunch fresh cilantro

¼ lime

½ head leafy green lettuce

JUICE 4: ULCERS

¼ head red cabbage

2 carrots

½ unpeeled Granny Smith apple, seeds removed

JUICE 5: ARTHRITIS, DIABETES, ECZEMA

2 carrots

2 celery stalks

1 small or medium cucumber

⅛ bunch fresh flat-leaf parsley

JUICE 6: HEART DISEASE AND CANCER

1 carrot

1 (¼-inch piece) fresh ginger

⅛ bunch fresh parsley

2 kale leaves

JUICE 7: BLOOD PRESSURE AND BLOOD PURIFIER

½ medium beet

2 carrots

3 celery stalks

JUICE 8: BODY CLEANSING

1 unpeeled Granny Smith apple, seeds removed

1 carrot

1 (½-inch piece) fresh ginger

JUICE 9: LIVER FUNCTION AND MEMORY

¼ unpeeled Granny Smith apple, seeds removed

1 fennel bulb

1 (¼-inch piece) fresh ginger

8 fresh peppermint leaves

JUICE 10: PREMATURE AGING AND SKIN

6 or 7 fresh basil leaves

1 medium cucumber

½ pint strawberries

JUICE 11: STRAWBERRY-CARROT KEFIR SMOOTHIE

½ cup organic strawberries

2 organic carrots

1 (½-inch piece) fresh ginger

4 ounces goat milk kefir

Juice the first 3 ingredients and mix with cold kefir.

Canine Only

The bulk recipes that follow are nutrient-dense, yet certain supplements may still be required for your dog. So check with your veterinarian about your particular pup.

We all want to eat complete balanced diets with top-quality ingredients, but if you or your dog can't digest or absorb the nutrients, you are wasting money and food. In order to digest and absorb the nutrients you need for good health, you and your dog need good bacteria and enzymes.

We may not have enough of these life-giving critters in our gut due to modern lifestyles, the way we eat and drink, the air we breathe, and the medicines we take. You and your dog need to have plenty of probiotics and enzymes to digest food and absorb nutrients; in addition, they perform another thousand tasks necessary to keep your immune system in tip-top shape.

Below are some suggestions on how to supplement your dog's diet, and what is required for the important function of digestion.

Probiotics

Dr. Ohhira's Probiotic is one of the best probiotic supplements on the market. Mimi, Mister Casper, and I take them faithfully, and if Mimi grabs anything off the street and swallows it, then Mimi may get two capsules. Mister Casper is above eating anything off the street. He won't even drink tap water. He likes only filtered water with a few drops of Cell Food. We usually take his special water to the park with us. Casper is allergic to many things so Dr. Ohhira's probiotics are a necessity.

Also we use goat milk or coconut kefir; both are delicious. You can buy them at most health food stores in the refrigerated section.

The food that these guys really love is green tripe; but it stinks so bad! It has all the probiotics and enzymes that a ruminant animal needs to digest food, and it will help your Fido to digest his food, too. Go online and find where you can locally purchase green tripe. Be sure you feed the green tripe to them raw. If you cook it, all the health-promoting benefits from the bacteria and enzymes will be destroyed. Get over the smell for the health of your dog. The good thing is your dog will love it, and it will be gone in seconds so you don't have to worry about it *stinking* around.

Enzymes

Digestive enzymes aid in ensuring that your dog will get the most benefit from his food. However, enzymes do much more than help with digestion; they also help boost his immune system, and help detoxify and clean up the blood.

There are two digestive enzymes products I've found for dogs that really do a nice job. I have used both of these products for Mimi and Casper and they are both excellent.

Mercola Digestive Enzymes for Pets has animal enzymes that help the animal break down his food more like he was designed to do in the wild. *Rx Zyme* by RX Vitamins is a complete digestive enzyme.

Raw Ground Beef Dinner

Ingredients

2 pounds ground beef

4 to 5 chicken livers

3 zucchini

¼ cup sunflower seed sprouts

3 to 4 broccoli florets

¼ bunch fresh cilantro, chopped

10 to 12 sugar snap peas

1 tablespoon flax meal

1½ tablespoons nutritional yeast

1½ teaspoons bonemeal

Place all the ingredients except for the ground meat in a food processor and process until blended thoroughly. Add the meat and mix in by hand. The mixture will keep in the refrigerator for about 4 days, or freeze in individual servings.

Raw Grass-Fed Chuck Roast with Green Beans and Tomato Sauce

Ingredients

    16 ounces French green beans (haricot verts), cut in half crosswise

    1 red bell pepper, seeded and chopped

    2 to 3 pounds grass-fed chuck roast, cut into ½-inch cubes

    1 (15-ounce) can low-sodium organic tomato sauce

    1 teaspoon dried oregano

    1 tablespoon coconut oil

    1½ teaspoons bonemeal

In a steamer, steam the green beans and bell peppers for about 5 minutes. Cool and purée.

In a large bowl, mix together the cubed meat, tomato sauce, oregano, coconut oil, and bonemeal by hand. Add the puréed green beans.

Store in individual servings in the refrigerator for about 5 days, or freeze.

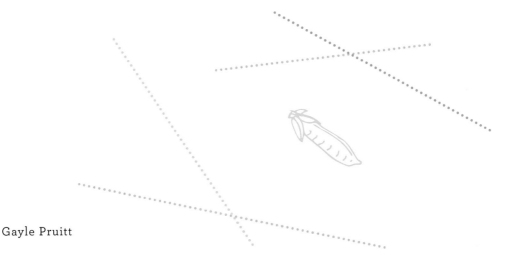

Raw Brisket

Ingredients

    6 to 7 pounds beef brisket, chopped

    1½ pounds carrots, peeled and sliced into 2-inch coins

    4 celery stalks, cut into 2-inch pieces

    1 bottle Lakewood Organic Super Veggie Juice (the only bottled juice I've found with no onions)

    3 heads green leafy lettuce, chopped

    1 tablespoon bonemeal

Trim off the fat, leaving a ¼-inch layer, and cut the brisket into small cubes.

Purée the carrots, celery, and lettuce with the tomato juice in a food processor. Stir in the chopped meat and bone meal by hand.

Freeze in individual servings.

If you have a grinder, you may find this recipe a healthy option for your dogs. For medium and small dogs this would be a month's supply or more.

If you don't have a grinder, make smaller portions more often.

This is a versatile recipe; you can change the vegetables and meat for variety.

Bulk Meat Grinder Raw Food (Large Quantity Yield)

Ingredients

30 pounds raw chicken neck

5 to 6 pounds raw beef hearts, chopped

3 pounds beef or chicken livers

5 cans sardines, packed in water, rinsed of salt and drained

3 fennel bulbs, with stem and fronds, chopped

4 to 5 zucchini, chopped

4 bell peppers, (red, yellow, orange, and/or green), seeded and chopped

4 heads romaine lettuce, chopped

2 apples, seeds and cores removed (seeds are toxic to your dog!)

1 cooked acorn squash, seeds included, outer skin removed

2 cups sprouted sunflower seeds, loosely packed

½ cup coconut oil, or extra-virgin olive oil

½ cup raw pumpkin seeds

¼ cup eggshell calcium or bonemeal (I use Now brand bonemeal)

¼ cup nutritional yeast

3 tablespoons ground fennel seeds

2 tablespoons peeled and minced fresh ginger

1 tablespoon dried dill

1 tablespoon mild paprika

3 tablespoons chia seeds (optional)

Grind and completely mix all the ingredients. Place in individual serving containers and freeze. To thaw, place individual servings in the refrigerator overnight to use the following day.

Cooked

All dogs, like humans, are unique in their likes, dislikes, and their nutritional needs, so please ask your veterinarian what is best for your dog. For these recipes, you may purée the meat and lightly steam all the vegetables if your dog has irritable bowel syndrome (IBS).

Cooked Roast

Ingredients

- 2 pounds cooked beef roast
- 1 pound cooked beef heart, chopped (boil in water for 10 minutes, then chop)
- ¼ pound beef liver, chopped (boil with beef heart)
- 3 small cans sardines or 1 large can, packed in water, rinsed of salt
- 3 large carrots, chopped
- 3 celery stalks, chopped
- 2 collard green leaves
- 1 cup frozen peas
- ¼ cup flat-leaf parsley
- 1 cup fresh or frozen cranberries
- 2 tablespoons chia seeds, soaked
- 2 tablespoons coconut oil
- 1 tablespoon lecithin
- 2 tablespoons nutritional yeast
- 2 teaspoons eggshell calcium

Place all the ingredients except for the chopped meat in a food processor and process until blended thoroughly. Add the meat and mix in by hand. The mixture will keep in the refrigerator for about 4 days, or freeze in individual servings.

Makes 4 pounds

Dirty Dog

Ingredients

2 cups homemade chicken broth (no onions)

1 pound beef hearts, chopped

¼ pound chicken or beef livers, chopped

½ teaspoon mild paprika

3 tablespoons olive oil

1 large green bell pepper, seeded and chopped

1 large red bell pepper, seeded and chopped

4 celery stalks, strings removed, coarsely chopped

1 pound ground beef (labeled 90 percent lean)

1 cup chopped parsley

Heat the chicken stock in a 12-quart stockpot and add the hearts and livers along with the paprika. Cover and simmer gently for 15 minutes.

In a large skillet over medium-high heat, warm the oil. Add the peppers and celery and sauté until tender. Remove from the skillet.

Add the ground beef to the skillet and sauté until lightly browned. Drain the meat in a colander and discard the fat.

Remove the livers and hearts from the chicken broth, and reserve the broth. Cool the livers and hearts, place in a food processor, and pulse for about 1 minute. Add the liver and heart mixture, along with the browned meats, to the vegetables. Place all the ingredients in to the stockpot and add ½ cup of the reserved chicken broth. Cover and simmer for 15 to 20 minutes. Gently stir in the parsley. Freeze in individual servings.

Makes about 3½ pounds

Chicken Breast with Spinach and Red Peppers

....

This recipe is ideal for the dog that has a hard time metabolizing fat.

Ingredients

    4 large chicken breasts, skinned, cooked, and chopped (about 3½ pounds)

    1 to 2 packets giblets containing chicken heart, liver, and gizzards, cooked and chopped

    1 (1-pound) bag frozen spinach, thawed and cooked

    4 red bell peppers, roasted and seeded

    1½ teaspoons coconut oil

    1 tablespoon flaxseed meal

    1 cup cooked quinoa

    2 teaspoons bonemeal

Place all the ingredients except for the chicken breast and giblets in a food processor and process until blended thoroughly. Add the meat and mix in by hand. The mixture will keep in refrigerator for about 4 days, or freeze in individual servings.

Makes 4 pounds dog food

Cooked Turkey Dinner (Large Quantity Bulk Food)

Ingredients

Boned meat from a large poached turkey, skin removed (see recipe for
Turkey in a Pot, page 29)

1 pint chicken livers, boiled for 8 to 10 minutes

2 (14½-ounce) cans wild-caught salmon, with skin and bones

3 large sweet potatoes, cooked

2 cups cooked quinoa

1 pound blanched green beans

2 heads leafy lettuce, chopped

¼ bunch parsley

1½ cups fresh or frozen cranberries

1 tablespoon dried rubbed sage

1 tablespoon ground turmeric

2½ tablespoons chia seeds, soaked

¼ cup nutritional yeast

3 tablespoons coconut oil

2 tablespoons lecithin (optional)

2½ tablespoons eggshell calcium or bonemeal

Place all the ingredients except for the turkey and salmon in a food processor and process until blended thoroughly. Add the turkey and salmon and mix in by hand. The mixture will keep in the refrigerator for about 4 days, or freeze in individual servings.

Makes 25 pounds dog food

Cooked Ground Turkey and Summer Squash Dinner

Ingredients

  2 tablespoons coconut oil

  2 teaspoons fennel seeds

  3 pounds ground turkey thigh meat

  2 small zucchini

  2 small yellow crookneck squash

  1 fennel bulb, chopped

  3 cups mixed spring greens

  1 ounce fresh blueberries

In a large hot skillet over medium–high heat, warm the coconut oil. Add the fennel seeds and ground turkey and cook for about 15 minutes, or until the turkey has turned a light brown. Set aside to cool.

Add the rest of the ingredients to a food processor and purée. Mix the puréed vegetables with the cooled turkey mixture by hand. Store the mixture in the refrigerator for up to 5 days, or freeze in individual servings.

Mimi's Seaweed Muffins

Ingredients

   1½ cups cooked millet

   2 sheets nori seaweed, cut into strips

   ¼ cup wakame flakes (seaweed)

   3 large eggs, whisked

   1 tablespoon melted coconut oil

Preheat the oven to 375 degrees.

Place all the ingredients except for the coconut oil in a bowl and stir until just combined; do not overmix. Brush mini muffin cups with the melted oil. Fill the cups with the mixture and bake for 20 minutes. Transfer to a rack and cool for 10 minutes. These muffins freeze well.

Makes 24 mini muffins

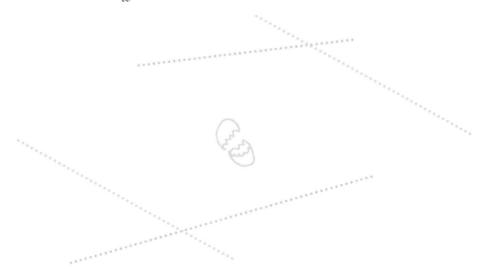

Acorn Squash, Quinoa, and Cinnamon Mini Muffins

Ingredients

    1 cup cooked acorn squash

    1 cup cooked quinoa (see recipe page 31)

    3 large eggs, whisked

    2 tablespoons kefir (I use goat milk kefir)

    1½ teaspoons ground cinnamon

    1 tablespoon coconut oil, melted

Preheat the oven to 375 degrees.

Place all the ingredients except for the coconut oil in a bowl and stir until completely mixed. Do not overmix.

Brush the muffin cups with coconut oil. Spoon the squash mixture into the muffin cups, filling the cups completely.

Bake for 20 minutes. Remove from the oven, transfer to a wire rack, and cool for 10 minutes. These muffins freeze well.

Makes 24 mini muffins

Acorn Squash and Coconut Mini Muffins

Ingredients

    1 cup cooked acorn squash

    ½ cup shredded unsweetened coconut

    1 cup quinoa, cooked with coconut oil

    3 large eggs, whisked

    2 tablespoons kefir (I use goat milk kefir)

    1½ teaspoons ground cinnamon

    1 tablespoon coconut oil, melted

Preheat the oven to 375 degrees.

Place all the ingredients except for the coconut oil in a bowl and stir until completely mixed. Do not overmix.

Brush the mini muffin cups with coconut oil. Spoon the squash mixture into the muffin cups, filling them completely. Bake for 20 minutes. Remove from oven, transfer to a wire rack, and let cool for 10 minutes.

Makes 24 mini muffins

Turkey, Millet, and Cranberry Muffins

I use this muffin recipe after Thanksgiving or Christmas when I have leftover roast turkey with cranberry-millet dressing.

Ingredients

    1 cup millet-cranberry dressing (See millet recipe, page 31)

    1 cup cooked roast turkey, finely chopped

    4 medium eggs, whisked

    1 tablespoon coconut oil, melted

Preheat the oven to 370 degrees.

Put all the ingredients in a bowl and stir until just mixed. Do not overmix.

Brush the mini muffin cups with melted coconut oil and fill them ¾ full with batter. Bake for 20 minutes.

Transfer to a wire rack and cool for 10 minutes. These muffins freeze well.

Makes 32 mini muffins

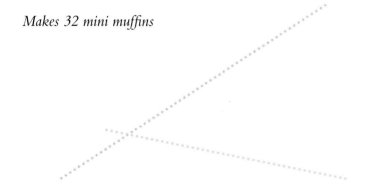

Vegetable and Quinoa Muffins

Ingredients

    1 cup cooked quinoa

    ½ red bell pepper, seeded and minced

    1 small carrot, minced

    ¼ cup green beans, minced

    2 tablespoons flat-leaf parsley, chopped finely

    Dash of sea salt

    4 medium eggs, whisked

    ½ teaspoon baking soda

    1 tablespoon melted butter

Preheat the oven to 370 degrees.

Put all the ingredients in a bowl and stir until just mixed. Do not overmix. Brush the mini muffin cups with the melted butter and fill the cups completely. Bake for 20 minutes. Transfer to a wire rack and cool for 10 minutes. These muffins freeze well.

Makes 24 mini muffins

   Gayle Pruitt

Yummy Chicken Liver Squares

Ingredients

    1 pint raw chicken livers (do not drain)

    1 carrot, finely chopped or shredded

    1 tablespoon coconut oil

    ½ teaspoon ground turmeric

    ½ teaspoon celery seeds

    ¼ teaspoon ground cloves

    1½ cups gluten-free, all-purpose flour

    1 teaspoon olive or coconut oil

Preheat the oven to 350 degrees.

Line a baking sheet with parchment paper. Add all the ingredients to a food processor and process until smooth; the mixture will be thick yet pourable. Brush a small amount of oil on a baking sheet and put a piece of parchment paper over the baking sheet. Pour the entire mixture on top of the parchment paper and smooth until the mixture is about a ¼ inch thick.

Bake for 25 to 30 minutes, depending on how crunchy you want the squares.

Transfer to a wire rack to cool. Place the squares in an airtight container. They will keep, refrigerated, for about 2 weeks, or you may also freeze them.

Makes about 30 squares

Chicken, Blackberry, and Millet Squares

Ingredients

1 bone-in, chicken breast

¼ cup fresh blackberries

2 cups millet flour

1 tablespoon coconut oil

1 teaspoon ground cinnamon

1 teaspoon ground Turmeric

½ teaspoon ground cloves

2 cups chicken broth (no onions), or use the water you boiled the chicken in

1 teaspoon any oil

Preheat the oven to 350 degrees.

Add all the ingredients to a food processor and process until smooth; the mixture will be thick yet pourable.

Brush a small amount of any oil on a baking sheet and put a piece of parchment paper over the baking sheet. Pour the entire mixture on top of the parchment paper and smooth until the mixture is about ¼ inch thick.

Bake for 25 to 30 minutes, depending on how crunchy you want the squares.

Transfer to a wire rack to cool. Place the squares in a container. They will keep, refrigerated, for about 2 weeks, or you may freeze them.

Makes approximately 50 squares

Vegan Squares

Ingredients

- 1 cup overcooked lentils
- 2 carrots, chopped
- ½ cup fresh or frozen cranberries
- 2 cups cooked quinoa flour
- 1½ cups vegetable broth (no onions)
- ½ teaspoon ground cinnamon
- ½ teaspoon ground cardamom
- ¼ teaspoon ground cloves
- 1 teaspoon oil

Preheat the oven to 350 degrees.

Line a baking sheet with parchment paper. Add all the ingredients to a food processor and process until smooth; the mixture will be thick yet pourable. Brush a small amount of any oil on a baking sheet and put a piece of parchment paper over the baking sheet. Pour the entire mixture on top of the parchment paper and smooth until the mixture is about ¼ inch thick.

Bake for 25 to 30 minutes depending on how crunchy you want the squares.

Transfer to a wire rack to cool. Place the squares in an airtight container, they will keep, refrigerated, for about 2 weeks. You may also freeze them.

Makes 50 squares

Beefy Red Hearts

Ingredients

    2 cups Lakewood Organic Super Veggie Juice (no onions)

    3 or 4 ice cubes

    7 envelopes Knox gelatin

    1 pint beef broth (no onions)

Pour the juice into a bowl and add the ice cubes. Sprinkle the gelatin over the juice; stir and let stand for 2 minutes.

In a saucepan, bring the beef broth to a boil. Add the gelatin mixture and stir until the gelatin has dissolved, about 5 minutes.

Place in a rectangular glass baking dish and refrigerate until firm, about 3 hours.

Cut in squares or use a heart-shaped cookie cutter.

Makes approximately 20 to 24 squares

Christmas Vegetable Squares

Ingredients

- 1 cup frozen cranberries
- 1 cup frozen spinach
- ¾ cup cold water
- 7 envelopes plain gelatin
- 1 quart chicken broth (no onions)
- 1 cup carrot strips, peeled from 2 carrots
- 2 cups blanched green beans, sliced into 1-inch pieces
- 1 pint ricotta cheese

Reserve a few cranberries for garnish. Put the remaining cranberries and frozen spinach in a bowl along with the cold water. Sprinkle the gelatin into the bowl with the cranberries and spinach. Stir so all the gelatin is submerged.

In a large saucepan, bring the chicken broth to a boil. Add the carrots, green beans, and cheese and stir. Reduce the heat to low, add the gelatin mixture and stir until dissolved.

Pour into a 2-inch deep rectangular glass dish. Sprinkle in the reserved cranberries. Refrigerate for about 3 hours, or until firm. Cut into squares.

Makes sixteen 2-inch squares; cut in half for smaller dogs.

Jerky

Jerky is an ancient meat-preparation technique with a broad history. Native Americans sun-dried their meat with salt and herbs. The Spanish conquistadors cut the meat into strips and hung the strips up in their ships to air-dry. They called their dried meat *charqui*. The natives tried to say *charqui* but with their accent it came out "jerky."

In the thirteenth century, Mongol horsemen led by Genghis Khan would place strips of meat between the horse and their saddle. When dinner time came around they would reach up under the saddle and take the meat out. It would be nice and warm, salty, and tenderized.

Casper, Mimi, and I prepare our jerky a little differently. It would be easier in a dehydrator but we use the oven. None of our friends own a dehydrator and they can be expensive.

Sweet Potato "Jerky"

Ingredients

    2 large, unpeeled sweet potatoes, washed and cut into ¼-inch slices

    1 teaspoon ground cinnamon (helps with blood sugar)

    ½ teaspoon ground fenugreek (optional; good for digestion)

Preheat the oven to 175 degrees.

Mix the cinnamon and fenugreek together and sprinkle over the sweet potato slices. Line a baking sheet with parchment paper and arrange the slices on the paper. Bake for 3 hours, or until totally dry and leathery.

Remove from the oven and allow to cool; then place in a plastic bag. The jerky will keep in the refrigerator for about 2 weeks (if it lasts that long).

Makes about 12

Beef Heart "Jerky"

Ingredients

    1 beef heart, cut into thin strips 1 to 2 inches wide and 1/8 inch thick

    1 tablespoon ground cumin (an anticarcinogenic)

    1 teaspoon ground ginger (for digestion; also an anti-inflammatory)

Preheat the oven to 150 degrees. Wash the beef heart strips and pat dry. Put the ground cumin and ground ginger in a plastic bag, add beef heart strips, and shake.

Line a baking sheet with parchment paper, and arrange the beef heart strips on the paper. Bake for 8 to 10 hours, or overnight, until completely dry. Transfer to a wire rack to cool. When cool, place in a plastic bag. The jerky will keep in the refrigerator for 2 weeks, or in the freezer for 6 months.

Makes approximately 8 to 10 strips

Gayle Pruitt

Chicken Breast "Jerky"

Ingredients

- 2 chicken breast fillets, cut into thin strips 1 to 2 inches wide and 1/8 inch thick
- 1 tablespoon ground turmeric (an anti-inflammatory)
- 1 quart water
- 1 teaspoon coconut oil

Preheat the oven to 175 degrees. Add the turmeric to a bowl of water along with the chicken strips and let soak for about 20 minutes. Pat dry. Lightly grease baking sheet with coconut oil, or place a lightly greased piece of parchment paper on the baking sheet. Place the dry strips on the baking sheet and bake for 2 to 2½ hours. Transfer to a wire rack to cool. When cool, place in a plastic bag. The jerky will keep in the refrigerator for up to 2 weeks, or in the freezer for 6 months.

Makes approximately 10 to 12 strips

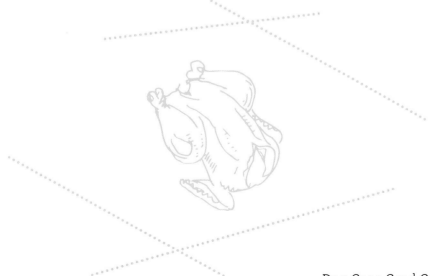

THE LAST WORD

Keep your weight and your dog's weight under control. Obesity in you and in your dog is a prescription for trouble. When overweight, both humans and dogs are more at risk for many lifestyle illnesses such as heart disease, diabetes, and even certain cancers. Being overweight is also hard on your joints, messes up your hormones, and depletes your energy. So exercise, and eat the right foods to be able to enjoy life to its fullest.

When you exercise, it doesn't take long for you and your dog to feel the benefits. The right kind of exercise strengthens the heart and lungs, builds muscle, and helps rid the body of toxins, including the bad estrogens that can cause trouble. Exercise increases circulation, which brings more oxygen to the cells and tissues. Increased activity burns calories that, in turn, burn fat, and you lose weight. But that's not all! For a big bonus, exercise affects the brain in many different, positive ways; it helps with perception, memory, judgment, and reasoning. It lifts your mood, and eases your pain.

Now that you and your dog buddy have more energy and are excited about life, you will burn even more calories and fat.

Next in the equation is water. Remember, pure water for you and your dog keeps the toxins away. Please don't let your best buddy drink from puddles on the street. It's not just the bacteria that is the problem. Lead, arsenic, and other poisons could be out on the road. They are all carcinogenic. Change your dog's water at least once a day. Get a good water filter. The money spent is well worth it in the savings on your veterinarian and doctor bills.

The quality of the air that we breathe is also very important. Air in the parks and in the backyard is great, but not the air on the highway. The air in our home needs to be as pure as possible, so nix those toxic cleaning chemicals. Get an air purifier. If you can't afford a good air purifier then buy some potted or hanging plants that will also take many toxins out of the air and will help with allergies, too.

Next, use natural products for you and your dog. There are so many wonderful natural flea and tick powders, shampoos, and sprays that do not have side effects. There is no reason now to use harsh chemicals on yourself or on your canine kids. The same goes for lawn products. You don't need to use toxic chemicals in your yard and landscaping. There are many natural alternatives that do a wonderful job. Listen to Howard Gavrett, The Dirt Doctor, at www.dirtdoctor.com.

Keep your life and your dog's life as simple as possible. Try to remove as much stress from your life as you can. There could be people in your life who are toxic. Stay away from them. Life is too precious and too short; you must make smart choices. You will never be able to change toxic people. They are who they are and if they want to change, great, but you can't do it for them. That's not your job. Your job is for you to be happy and healthy and make a happy, healthy life for your dog.

One more little thing: Ask yourself, "Do I run to the doctor every time I get the sniffles and ask for medication?" If you do, you are contributing to the toxic impact on your life. Our immune system can handle most of our issues. Of course, when you do get sick by all means go to your doctor. And if your dog is really sick, go to the veterinarian. But if you don't have to have drugs, don't press your doctor or the veterinarian into giving them to you. If the doctor does prescribe a drug, it doesn't hurt to ask your doctor what the side effects are and how necessary the drug is. Remember: Every single drug has a side effect, and the more drugs you take, the more side effects you may suffer and the more drugs will be prescribed to take care of those side effects. What a vicious cycle!

Food for you and your dog needs to be as clean as possible. By that, I mean buy organic and/or locally grown meat and eggs. Find pasture-fed or, at the very least, antibiotic and hormone free. Buy organic vegetables and fruits. And please stay away from sugar (a real killer), wheat, corn, and most soy and dairy.

Mimi, Casper, and I say "Bone Appetite" and have a wonderful life!

Index

Note: Recipes followed by ★ are for canines only.